10644823

"An exhilarating adventure on m̶ ̶ ̶ ̶ ̶ ̶ ̶ worth reading.
- Christopher Luzzio, MD, Neurologist,
University of Wisconsin Hospital and Clinics

"From the taking a single footstep to the climbing of Mt. Kilimanjaro, these stories teach us what it means to lose locomotion and what it feels like to get it back."
- Erik Belgum, Author of
Star Fiction and *Collected Stort Shories (SIC)*

"This is more than a book about undaunting leadership. It is a book about the beauty of the human spirit. You must read it."
- Edward Grinnan, Editor-in-Chief, *Guideposts*,
and author of *The Promise of Hope: How True Stories of Hope and Inspiration Saved My Life and How They Can Transform Yours.*

"*More than a Mountain* is just that. It leads us to the summit of Kilimanjaro and into the lives of a unique group of people with a common goal. Their individual accounts affirm the truth that mountains are not obstacles in our way but pathways to empowerment."
- Todd Burleson, President,
Alpine Ascents International

"This book shows the beauty of the mountains–and the daunting challenge they pose. Everybody's limits are different. This book is a wonderful testimony to mustering courage in the search for those limits, and an inspiration to living a life that is as full as can be. "
- Peer Baneke, CEO,
Multiple Sclerosis International Federation

"I think of the Chinese proverb, "The person who says it cannot be done should not interrupt the person doing it." Frankly, I wouldn't have thought it was possible for someone with MS to scale Mount Everest, let alone the highest peak on each of the seven continents. Then, Lori Schneider leads fourteen people with MS or Parkinson's up Mount Kilimanjaro. What? The only way I can make sense out of that is to accept that Lori has redefined the word "possible." Without question, these stories will inspire you and leave you in awe of the power and beauty of the human spirit."

- Phil Bolsta, author of *Through God's Eyes: Finding Peace and Purpose in a Troubled World*

"It's a rare individual who has not faced personal tragedy, but it is equally as rare to find one who has come through on the other side a stronger and more complete person. The stories in *More than a Mountain* are of just such individuals, those who pushed beyond the limits of their own strength to overcome the physical and emotional effects of disease, loss, addiction, and other personal pain to forge a new self not defined by their tragedy."

- Mary Stirrat, reporter for The Inter-County Leader

"We all have our mountains to climb; be they literal or figurative ones. *More than a Mountain* is a beautiful telling of how neurological challenges can be faced when patients, loved ones and physicians join together. The healing community that results is extraordinarily powerful."

- James Bowen, MD, Medical Director, Multiple Sclerosis Center, Swedish Neuroscience Institute

"Each and every one of the Leap of Faith climbers summited far more than a 19,000' peak. The intimate stories of determination, fear, and faith shared in *More than a Mountain* are a testament that engaging in life requires a Leap of Faith taken by each climber to define life rather than let a disease or condition define their lives. Whether a physician, seasoned adventurer with MS or a loving spouse of a determined husband with Parkinson's the Leap of Faith climbers are a keen reminder that actively engaging life is the key to a life well lived and provides the footprints and courage for others to follow. Definitely an inspirational must read!"

- Cheryl Siefert, Executive Director,
Parkinson Association of the Rockies

"No member of this remarkable team should ever think of themself as 'ordinary' again. Each candid account of the challenges overcome to successfully climb Mt. Kilimanjaro is a testament to the extraordinary power of the conscious choice to believe "I CAN!" This book trumps fictional tales of superheroes or adventure any day. It's a must-read for anyone of any age who either doubts their true potential or desires to achieve it."

- Michele Hermansen, Photojournalist,
Global Justice Advocate

"I have read all the exciting books by Krauker and Viesturs regarding climbing; *More than a Mountain* can be proudly shelved next to them. The courage, fortitude and persistence of all the climbers underscores their passion for life and for the fighting of disease that is continually trying to rob them of control. Bigger than the climb and the summit, is that every person, healthy or those fighting a neurological disease, can identify their own mountain and go out and conquer it on a daily basis."

- Dr. Jay L. Alberts,
President and Founder, Pedaling for Parkinsons

"*More than a Mountain* is more than a collection of climbing stories. A loose knit team of climbers, many with MS and PD took one of life's largest challenges by climbing Mt. Kilimanjaro. Their personal stories make you think about your own limitations and what is stopping you from going forward."

- Alan Arnette, Mountaineer,
Alzheimer's Advocate and Speaker

"As you put perceived obstacles behind you, your ascent to fearlessness will be achieved. This book serves as a reminder that anything is possible."

- Stephanie Wautier, RN, BSN, DC

"*More than a Mountain* is a textbook in life enrichment. It demonstrates the capacity of the human spirit to triumph over the loss experienced with the onset of chronic illness and the ability to find true fulfillment through achieving something extraordinary against the odds. By conquering the physical challenges of Kilimanjaro, Lori and her fellow climbers also conquered their own physical adversities, revealing the importance of inner strength in defining our enjoyment of life. Read and be inspired."

- Tom Isaacs, Co-founder,
The Cure Parkinson's Trust

More than a MOUNTAIN

Our Leap of Faith

More than a Mountain: Our Leap of Faith

Book Cover Designer: Susie Weber
Book Cover Photograph: Jeff Rennicke
Editing: Donna Mazzitelli, Writing with Donna
Layout/Design: Andrea Costantine
Photographs: Jeff Rennicke
Hill Country Font: S. John Ross
More than a Mountain Theme Song:
Gina Anderson, Suz Thomson
Kilimanjaro Crest Designer: Nancy Gardner

Printed in the United States of America

First Edition
ISBN: 978-1-48104-846-0

More than a MOUNTAIN

Our Leap of Faith

Foreword by Jeff Rennicke
Introduction by Lori Schneider

First-hand Accounts by the Leap of Faith Climbers
Supporting multiple sclerosis and Parkinson's disease

Dedication

To all those who are climbing mountains and obstacles in their own lives and those living with multiple sclerosis and Parkinson's disease.

Contents

Foreword:
To Carry the Light

Jeff Rennicke

IN THE PREDAWN LIGHT OF JULY 18, 2011, CLIMBERS from the "Leap of Faith Expedition" stood at the summit of 19,340-foot Mount Kilimanjaro. The morning air atop Africa's highest point was soft blue and cold. As the sun rose that morning, an orange glow illuminated their faces. A sharp wind ripped the tears from their eyes. Down coats and thick mitts muffled the celebratory hugs and high-fives. For most climbers and the majority of expeditions, this would have been the proudest moment, the culmination of years of pre-trip planning and logistics, the months of grueling training hikes, days of burning leg muscles and lung-searing effort of the climb itself. The summit moment is often the single most important reason most climbers climb and the whole purpose of the expedition itself. But not this time. These were not most climbers and Leap of Faith was not one of the majority of expeditions.

On another morning more than a decade earlier, expedition leader Lori Schneider had rolled out of bed to get on the treadmill, as she did every morning, when she noticed that the left side of her body was tingling, from her foot through her shoulders, half her face, even the left half of her tongue. "It was as if someone had drawn a line down the middle," she says, "and half of me had gone numb." At first she suspected a cortisone shot in her foot a few days earlier had hit a nerve, and she assumed the numbness would go away. It didn't.

Lori called her doctor, touching off a three-month barrage of tests—lupus, Lyme's disease, MRI's, and CT Scans. On an around-the-world trip a few years earlier she'd eaten a lot of wild game. "I was pretty relieved when the test for warthog came back negative," she jokes. But some of the other potential causes were not as humorous. The numbness soon spread to parts of her right side and doctors began to suspect a stroke or brain cancer. Eventually, doctors came to a diagnosis: multiple sclerosis.

Multiple sclerosis (or MS) affects over 2.5 million people worldwide, attacking the central nervous system, causing scarring on the brain, the spinal cord, even the optic nerves. It can result in loss of mobility, loss of vision, as well as cognitive difficulties, even paralysis. Called "the crippler of young adults" because most of those diagnosed are between the ages of 20 and 50, MS has no cure.

"Those two little letters—MS—sent me into panic mode," Schneider says. She quit her 20-year career as a school teacher, ended her 22-year marriage, sold her home, and left her community of Steamboat Springs, Colorado. "I acted out of fear," she says. "I just ran from my whole life." She ran to the mountains.

"MS carries with it a real stigma," Schneider says. "I

remember watching those commercials as a kid: 'MS, the crippler of young adults.' My biggest fear was what the MS would do to the person I thought I was. I wanted to be judged by my personal strength and not by the label of this illness. Mountain climbing was a chance to show the world that people with MS can and do achieve things in their lives at, literally, the highest levels."

She began a quest—to be the first person with MS to stand atop the highest mountain on every continent. One by one, she conquered her fear and climbed. Alaska's Mount McKinley, Europe's Mt. Elbrus, Africa's Mount Kilimanjaro, Mount Vinson in Antarctica, Aconcagua in South America, and others. "As I climbed," Lori says," I thought about how many people with MS struggle just to walk across the living room, and here I was climbing mountains. Those were the people who empowered me, who gave me the courage to continue."

Finally, at 8:39 a.m. Nepal time on May 23, 2009, Lori Schneider became the first person with MS ever to stand atop Mount Everest and the first person with MS in history ever to complete the Seven Summits. On Everest's summit, she unfurled the World MS flag. "It was so windy I could barely hang on to it," she says, "but as I held that flag over the summit I thought, what a change in ten years. Here was this person who ten years ago thought her life was ending and now I'm standing literally on top of the world holding a flag that screams 'I have MS and I'm okay.'"

People ask her what it was like to be on top of the world, but for those ten surreal minutes on the world's highest summit, Schneider could not see a thing. No view at all, in the middle of the clouds and storm. With no outward view, all she could see was what was inside of her. "What I saw," she says, "was a person who had become brave since that terrifying day she woke up numb. I saw a person who was no longer afraid to live life passionately, who took a leap of faith and tried something that once would have scared her to death. I saw a person who had MS and hoped the world would see that those two little letters could also stand for 'Mostly Strong.'" And, she wanted to help others with MS see that too.

Today, Lori Schneider and her organization, Empowerment Through Adventure, inspires others with potential debilitating diseases to take their own leap of faith, climbing mountains of fear and doubt towards strength and renewal. The 2011 Leap of Faith: Mount Kilimanjaro expedition paired 14 climbers who had either MS or Parkinson's disease with 14 companion climbers. As with other expeditions, the summit loomed large in the hopes and dreams of the climbers. In the end, 21 of the 28 Leap of Faith team members would indeed make it to the top. But for all the men and woman on this trip, the climb had a higher purpose: to carry the light of hope and a message of strength to the highest reaches of both our planet and the human spirit.

These are their stories—stories of fear and pain, of the courage to dig deep into that well of strength that lies within us all, and the willingness to try and try again, even in the face of insurmountable odds. Here are stories of shared joy and faith, stories of people who are more than climbers, on a climb of a peak that was More than a Mountain, on an expedition that was more than a climbing journey. Here are the stories of a Leap of Faith.

Jeff Rennicke, *2011 Leap of Faith: Mount Kilimanjaro Expedition photographer. Jeff Rennicke is a nationally-known writer, speaker, and photographer. He is the author of 10 books, including* Treasures of Alaska *published by the National Geographic Society and more than 250 magazine articles. He lives in Bayfield, Wisconsin and acted as the photographer on the "Leap of Faith" expedition. More of his work can be seen at www.jeffrennicke.com.*

The Dream Begins

"As we work to create light for others,
we naturally light our own way."
- Mary Anne Radmacher

Introduction

Lori Schneider

LEAP OF FAITH: IDIOM-AMERICAN HERITAGE Dictionary. "A leap of faith, in its most commonly used meaning, is the act of believing in or accepting something intangible or unprovable. It is an act of complete trust in something that cannot readily be seen."

What does leap of faith mean to me? It is the driving force that possesses us to do something many others think of as foolish, outside of our reach, beyond the limits our labels have set for us, or those we have set in our own minds. It is that belief that we can achieve our goal, even when it is against all odds. It is the desire to try something that we know is probably impossible, but we try anyway. For me, it was attempting something that I never, ever, EVER thought was attainable and saying, "What have I got to lose?" Failure is only in the mind, and so is the ability to dream big.

My big dream started out as an ambition to set foot on each of the seven continents and experience the people, culture, and heartbeat of foreign lands. I began this dream by saving for a trip to Europe at age 15. I spent that summer living and traveling with a family in Germany and learning to immerse myself in another world. I came to understand that we can learn so much by stepping beyond our comfort level and challenging the mind and spirit. That first trip began a lifelong travel obsession that led me to Iceland, India, Russia, the Great Barrier Reef, the islands of Fiji, the Maldives and the Seychelles, Nepal, Vietnam, and Malaysia, just to name a few of the places. I even visited various countries in Africa during an eleven-week adventure via an overland truck.

In 1978, after graduating from an all women's college in Iowa, I began working as a special education and elementary education teacher in Colorado. My desire to impact children's lives through teaching lasted for 20 years and still continues today, as I encourage children and adults alike to dream big and not be afraid to try.

I have always maintained a strong connection with family and friends, and in 1993 I was inspired by my father's dream to climb Mt. Kilimanjaro in Africa. This led us to a successful summit of "Kili" on my dad's 61st birthday. He was my inspiration, my friend, and my hero. Six years later a second father-daughter climb of one of the world's highest peaks was set in motion. With a successful millennium summit of Mt. Aconcagua, South America's highest peak, my dream to climb the Seven Summits was born.

My desire to climb intensified in 1999, after my diagnosis of multiple sclerosis. Waking up with a body that was half numb, I feared the worst. I felt the panic of needing to complete my chosen task while I was still in control of my physical body. From that point on, I saved money when and where I could to pursue my passion of climbing. In 2000, I used what I had saved to participate in a climb of Nepal's highest non-technical trekking mountain, Mera Peak. Since I never truly believed I would be good enough to climb Mount Everest, Mera Peak was intended to be my substitute on the continent of Asia, or so I thought.

Next, I was off to Russia to climb Europe's highest peak, Mount Elbrus. With my health still strong, I trained on Mexican volcanoes for a climb of Mt. McKinley the following spring—or Denali as mountaineers call it. Thirty days of climbing, wearing a 60-pound pack as I dragged a 60-pound sled full of gear in the frigid Alaskan temperatures, would test my physical strength beyond anything I had ever experienced. With an investment of $10,000 in extreme weather gear, along with a determination that would not stop, I reached North America's highest peak in May of 2006.

Upon returning from the strenuous expedition on Denali, I was told that my persistent back pain was caused by a cyst on a nerve in my spine, which was being pinched between two disks. The cyst had developed from a slow leak of spinal fluid due to a faulty spinal tap done by a young medical student when I was first diagnosed. After back surgery and recovery time, followed by training to rebuild my strength, I was ready to move forward again.

With ice axe in hand and the desire to complete my dream of setting foot on each continent and climbing the Seven Summits, I climbed Australia's Mt. Kosciusko in July of 2008 and Mt. Vinson in Antarctica that November. I saved the best for last, and with my freshly-honed climbing skills and a renewed determination to give it my best shot, I set foot on the top of the world, Mt. Everest, on May 23, 2009.

I have been blessed in my life with many gifts, including opportunities to travel and climb. These experiences have enriched my life, and for that I am truly grateful. My biggest reward through all of this has been learning about overcoming fear and limitations and sharing these lessons with others. I formed a company called Empowerment Through Adventure, reaching out to those in need of a little courage of their own. It has been my dream to change the negative experience of being diagnosed with MS into one of growth and self-discovery. The goal of ETA is to empower others to move beyond their limitations and live their dreams.

Through my website, social media, speaking engagements, and adventure activities, I teach that ordinary people can achieve extraordinary things. I encourage others to take a leap of faith in their personal lives and climb their own mountains. We all have challenges to face, and our biggest obstacles are often the ones we place in our own path. When we move past our fears and rediscover our inner strength, we empower ourselves to move forward with courage. We learn that if we believe, oftentimes, we can achieve.

This desire to help others move beyond the mental mountains of fear and doubt was the driving force behind the Kilimanjaro Leap of Faith climb. I knew that climbing had given me the courage to face other obstacles in my own life with unwavering determination. Now it was my turn to help others move beyond their own perceived limitations of living with MS or Parkinson's disease.

I assembled a climbing team of 28 determined individuals, ranging in age from 23 to 79 years young— the oldest being my father. Each member had their own abilities, while 14 had a diagnosed disability of MS or PD. The remaining 14 joined the team as companion climbers, helping their partner every step of the way. Some had never visited a mountain in their life and few had ever climbed one before. All had a desire to take a leap of faith and challenge themselves to push beyond the normal parameters in their own lives. It was a chance to see what they were made of. It was also our chance as a team to shatter the world's perceptions of what is possible for a person with a neurodegenerative illness. It was time to show the world our abilities and see past our own disabilities. It was time to climb beyond our limits.

More than a Mountain is a collection of voices from those people who took a leap of faith together that dark summit night, on a mountain called Kilimanjaro. Kili at 19,340 feet is the largest free-standing mountain in the world and is a challenge for all. It tests the physical boundaries of the body and mental boundaries deep within one's soul. It challenges the endurance of the human spirit. In 2011, these 14 brave men and women with multiple sclerosis or Parkinson's disease, along with their supportive climbing companions, stepped outside of their individual comfort zones and took a leap. They made history. They leaped beyond what others thought possible for a person with a neurodegenerative disease. They trusted in the unknown, the unproven. They pushed their limits and each reached their own personal summits. For these 28 brave souls, Kilimanjaro truly was *More than a Mountain*. It was a Leap of Faith.

October 2012
Lori Schneider

Mount Kilimanjaro

Statistics

MOUNT KILIMANJARO, ONE OF THE SEVEN SUM-mits, stands on the border between Tanzania and Kenya as the "roof of Africa." Kili is the tallest freestanding mountain in the world. The summit of Uhuru Peak stands at 19,340 feet. There are seven routes to the summit: Shira, Lemosho, Machame, Umbwe, Mweka, Marangu, and Rongai. Our group took the Machame Route, also known as Whiskey Route. On this route the days are longer and the walks much steeper than the alternative routes, but it allows for more time to acclimatize.

Machame approaches from the southwest and descends using Mweka Route. Along the way climbers are rewarded with views of the Shira Plateau, an optional scramble up Lava Tower, a challenging climb up the Barranco Wall, and a traverse underneath Kilimanjaro's southern ice field. The descent occurs on the Mweka Route, a steep descent that is trouble for the knees and toes. Along the way climbers experience five different climate zones, beginning and ending in the rainforest and hitting the arctic zone on the summit, where temperatures can be well below zero.

Each year approximately 25,000 climbers attempt the summit of Kilimanjaro. According to the Kilimanjaro National Park statistics, only 41% of trekkers actually reach the summit, with the majority turning back at Gilman's Point, just 980 feet shy of the summit. There are a number of false summits in the last 1,500 vertical feet that can present both mental and physical obstacles to achieving the summit. Many attempt the climb under the misconception that it is easy because it does not require an individual to be a technical climber. Nothing could be further from the truth. Most are turned back from Kili or die because of acute mountain sickness from the high altitude. Multiple people die on the mountain each year. More have died on Kilimanjaro than on Everest, though fewer attempt Everest. For every 25,000 people who make the attempt to summit Kili, about 6 people die each year.

A note about environmental concerns: Alpine Ascents International, the company that led our climb, is committed to maintaining the ecosystems wherever they climb. They follow a "leave no trace" philosophy and ensure that everything taken in is carried back out. They also strive to assist the local population in protecting the land and people indigenous to the region. On their website they state, "The mountains are our home and we are unwilling to sacrifice the preservation for human objectives. On every one of our courses and climbs we teach and follow the environmentally appropriate Leave No Trace principles and practices." We were grateful to have them lead the way for us.

Changing Perceptions

"We must be willing to let go of the life we planned so as to have the life that is waiting for us."
- Joseph Campbell

Climbing Beyond
Our Limits

Lori Schneider

THE DAY I WOKE UP WITH A BODY HALF NUMB from multiple sclerosis was the day my life changed forever. I went from a whole person to a broken one with the placement of that one little foot on the floor. Nothing made sense in my life anymore, and I became a person who had lost a sense of self.

After wading through the tears and fears of what my life was to become, I stepped away a wounded person, with injuries so deep I felt they would never heal. I was bleeding from an open wound with no bandage to wrap around me. My heart was heavy, and my brain was aching from thoughts of what would become of me. I panicked and ran away from my life, fearing that I needed to gain independence while I still had my strength. I left my home, my husband, my job, my friends, and the sense of purpose that I once possessed. I slipped into the void of that deep emotional crevasse, unhooked from my safety lines that once would have pulled me back to reality.

As part of my need to escape my MS, I began to run at a pace that even I could hardly keep up with. I was determined to prove to myself that I was still in control of my physical body. Goals, which once would not have been important, seemed to drive me beyond my normal limits, especially physical ones.

Why mountain climbing, you might ask? How did this form of physical exertion stand out from all the other possibilities? I had always been drawn to the mountains and the peace they brought to my soul. And more than anything at the time, I needed peace. Climbing was also a test of endurance, of mind over matter, of pushing beyond my perceived limits. It seemed I also wanted to escape, which was based on a need to be isolated. In the mountains, I could hide. There, I insulated myself with others who were strong, possessing a "no excuse" attitude. Climbing gave me the time to think, to process all the carnage left after my runaway.

It wasn't until I stood on top of the highest point in South America, Mt. Aconcagua, that I reclaimed my life. It was a struggle to get to the summit set amidst a pile of scree and ice. My body was frozen, my vision was blurred, due to a burst blood vessel in my eye, and exhaustion had set in. As I stood by the cross marking the pinnacle on that millennium New Year's Eve, I made a decision that would impact my "new" life forever. I decided to let go of the shame I was feeling from carrying that label of MS. I decided that if I was strong enough to stand on top of a 22,840-foot mountain, I was strong enough to tell people I had MS. I was strong enough to face my life again without fear for the future. It was time to live again.

Over the next decade I climbed beyond my limits more than once. I was living and loving life again, and my scars were fading. The wounds that seemed so deep many years earlier were being stitched with memories of strength and joy. With the continental summits of Africa, South America, Europe, North America, and Australia under my belt, it was time to put my mental and physical strength to the test. What was I really made of? Could I live by the words I had shared with elementary and special education children so often during my twenty-year teaching career?

My goal as a teacher had been to help children believe in themselves and not be afraid to *try*. Now, it was my turn to learn those lessons. Was I strong enough to face a deadly mountain like Everest? What would take even more courage would be accepting the very real possibility that I might not make the summit. In attempting a goal as lofty as Everest, I had to give myself permission to try. I had to believe in myself in order to live my dreams. Sure, I knew that I might not always succeed at what I attempted, but I understood that there is no failure in that. The success is in the journey…it is *always* in the journey.

The day I took my leap of faith was the day that set the rest of my life in motion. It was in September of 2008. I was deep in thought about where I was going with this whole silly mountain climbing idea of mine. Could I actually complete my dream of climbing the Seven Summits? Who was I kidding? I had no formal mountaineering training to prepare me for the technical aspects I would face on Everest. I had used most of my savings to finance the first five of the Seven Summit climbs. I had no sponsors to believe in me and pave the way, just my own determination and drive.

I decided this day was going to be my day to leap and set wheels in motion to make the completion of my Seven

Summits dream a reality. I got out a marker and wrote Leap of Faith on the calendar. I circled it over and over to help embed the thought deep within my soul. Then, with only a "go for the gusto" attitude and a belief in myself, I sat down at the computer and composed a letter.

Dear Oprah, I am a 52 year-old woman trying to reinvent my life and live a dream. I have MS, but I am not afraid. I need help sharing my story so that I might someday begin to earn a living once again through speaking and raise the needed money to climb Mt Everest. Next...*Dear Dr. Phil*...Next....*Dear Jimmy Buffett*...Next...*Dear Today Show-Meredith Viera*... I typed with a fury of enthusiasm and courage, then stuffed each envelope with my letter, bio page, and climbing story. I hurried to the post office to mail them, before I could change my mind, and gave them a kiss for luck as I licked the stamps.

After days and weeks with no responses, I decided that I needed to take another approach. I signed up to climb the highest peak in Antarctica in November 2008 as well as Mt. Everest—the daddy of them all—in April 2009. After draining the last of my savings from the sale of my house to pay for the $40,000 Antarctica climb, I was broke. I went to the bank and asked for a loan to fund the $80,000 I would need for the Everest climb and supplemental oxygen to breathe at 29,035 feet. When I asked if I could take out a loan, they assumed I wanted the money for a car or home down payment. When I divulged that it was for a climb of Mt. Everest, they smiled and asked if my father would co-sign the loan. I *know* they thought a 52-year-old woman with MS was going to die trying and they would be stuck with a very large, unpaid debt. Dad signed, I sent in my payment to both climbing companies, and the course for the next year of my life was set.

I know the statistics show that climbing Mt. Everest is a dangerous proposition. People die. People are frozen in time on the side of a slope or deep in a crevasse, never to return. People are buried under walls of snow as daily avalanches scar the terrain. Yes, Everest was a scary place, I must admit. *So, why was I not afraid?* Seeing the body of the famous climber, Scott Fischer, frozen in the ice—as I made my way toward my goal—should have been enough to send me home, had I let in the fear. I needed to remind myself that fear would only put my mind in an unhealthy place and put my body in danger. So, I went to my mental "safety zone" while on Everest. I took all the love and support that had been sent my way along with me, every step of the way. As a result, I felt safe. My mantra was *Don't Let Fear In*.

The World MS Day organization heard about my story and asked if I would carry a flag in honor of the first World MS Day to the summit of Everest, should I be lucky enough to make it. It took two weeks for the flag to arrive via yak train to Everest Base Camp. The flag was stowed in my backpack and remained close to my heart during those weeks as we approached the summit. It gave me comfort and strength on days when I felt weak. I was carrying the hopes and dreams of all of us with MS in my pack.

On May 23, 2009, I became the first person with MS to summit Mt. Everest and complete the Seven Summits. It was an honor to carry that label of MS with me all the way to the top of the world. It was a chance to show the world that people with MS *can and do* achieve monumental things in their lives. It was also a chance for me to realize that my struggle over the label of MS had passed. I was no longer afraid.

Often, people ask me what it was like to be on top of the world. For those ten surreal minutes, I could not see a thing around me in the face of the clouds and storm. With no outward view all I could do was look inside of me. What I saw was a person who had become brave since that terrifying day she woke up numb. I saw a person who was no longer afraid to live life passionately—a person who took a leap of faith and tried something that once would have scared her to death. I saw a person with hope for the future, ready to embrace life, one step at a time.

Mt. Everest final journal entry:
May 25, 2009
Reinventing My Life
Daughter, Wife, Teacher, MS, Ex-wife,
Ex-Teacher, Mountain Climber

"As I reflect over the past two months climbing Everest, many times I feel small and insignificant in my world. Who would have thought as a little girl growing up playing with dolls that my life would have progressed to where I am now? As I have moved through the ages and stages in my life, I have felt the pain and pleasure of each of my 52 years. I am soft, tender, feminine, and yet wonderfully tough. I have reinvented my life over these past ten years.

I have gone from teaching young children to be brave and trust themselves to teaching myself these very lessons. Through these experiences in my life, I have begun to teach others as well. My lessons? Live Your Dreams…One Step at a Time…Trust… Take a Leap of Faith…Be Brave…Dream Big…and Believe in the Unbelievable."

Beyond Everest

For me, there are no more mountains that need to be scaled. I have climbed beyond the obstacles of fear and doubt, and my spirit has seen the view from the emotional summit. My dream for the future is to help others with disabilities and perceived limitations move beyond their own self-doubt.

This was the vision behind the Kilimanjaro Leap of Faith climb and the driving force behind my return to Africa. In 2011, the scene was the same, but the purpose of this second trip to Kilimanjaro was very different. This time, instead of strengthening my own soul, it was my dream to help others take a leap of faith in their own lives and believe in themselves once again.

Twenty-eight brave adventurers from all walks of life were ready to step outside of their comfort zone and take an emotional risk. Our team consisted of 10 people with multiple sclerosis, 4 living with Parkinson's disease, and 14 companions that helped each person climb beyond their perceived limitations. I knew this adventure would help put the *life* back in the lives of others who were facing illness and uncertainty. I knew this trip would give a sense of fulfillment to the companion climbers who were giving of their kind spirits through their participation and commitment. I knew this trip would be a chance for my father and me to conquer our third mountain together and bring our dream full circle from that first climb of Kilimanjaro together in 1993. What I did not expect was the profound impact each person's courage would have on me.

I watched a man with Parkinson's, who had two deep brain stimulators implanted in his scull, scale rock ledges all the while thinking about the risk his *companion* might face if he called on him for help. I witnessed teammates in their 60's putting one foot in front of the other for hours at a pace quicker than my own. I saw young women with a lifetime of dreams ahead of them struggling with elevation, bravely taking step after step into the darkness on summit night. Several had altitude sickness yet gave it their all in spite of nausea, diarrhea, asthma, muscle pain, and sheer exhaustion.

Companion climbers had nothing to gain but the satisfaction of helping someone else realize a dream. I witnessed medical personnel coming to the aid of everyone in need of a shoulder to lean on, both literally and figuratively. I saw my own father at 79 years young, training hard month after month and refusing to give up even when his body seemed tired or sore. Young comforting old, old comforting young, strong helping stronger, male and female not in competition, Parkison's assisting MS, MS assisting Parkinson's, husbands supporting wives, wives supporting husbands, person helping person—all became friends sharing one dream.

Each of us needed to rediscover the power we possessed

deep within. For me, I originally found that power through adventure. Now, I was finding power through the inspiration of others. For those on the Kilimanjaro Leap of Faith team, doubt was shattered, limitations were lifted, boundaries were broken, hearts were filled with joy, and empowerment was lived. Hear their stories of courage and inspiration. Kilimanjaro was more than a mountain for all of us. Together, we climbed a mountain called hope.

To all those living in fear…climb beyond your limits.

Lori Schneider is a mountain climber, dreamer, teacher, lifelong learner and inspirational speaker. She is one of approximately 38 women in the world to complete the Seven Summits—defined as reaching the highest peak on each continent—and one of only six women over the age of 50 to accomplish this feat. With her successful summit of Mt. Everest on May 23, 2009, she became the first person with multiple sclerosis to reach the top of the world and complete the Seven Summits. Through her company Empowerment Through Adventure, Lori shares her story and inspires people to be all that they can be and to live their own dreams, whatever they may be, one step at a time. Lori's message… if we believe, we can achieve.

Read more of Lori's story at:
www.EmpowermentThroughAdventure.com
www.facebook.com/EmpowermentThroughAdventure
Lori@ETAdventure.com

The Adventure that Changed My Perception of Disease

Sierra Farris

2010 WAS A SUCCESSFUL CLIMBING YEAR, FINALLY summiting Mt. Rainier after months of hard training. The year before, I had to turn back just below the summit due to unrelenting nausea and dizziness from altitude sickness. As exhilarating as climbing Mt. Rainier was, the sense of accomplishment quickly began to fade. During my time off from the rigors of training and climbing, I subsequently became captivated with the adventures of Dick Bass and Frank Wells and their quest to climb the highest peak on each continent.

Bass and Wells' stories of failed summit attempts, dangerous conditions, and logistical hurdles overcome by sheer determination to be the first to climb all seven summits was incredibly inspiring. I finished their novel and began my nightly Internet search for climbing videos. During my search one night in September, I came across Everest climber, Lori Schneider, who happened to have multiple sclerosis. I fought back tears of compassion as I watched a YouTube video about Lori's story of dealing with the diagnosis and symptoms of MS and her quest to climb the Seven Summits. I was amazed that a tiny woman with MS could manage such strenuous climbing in dangerous conditions that could barely be accomplished by two strong and healthy men.

Seeing for myself on a daily basis how my patients struggle to move or walk, I couldn't imagine the difficulties Lori must have encountered on her seven-summit quest. As a physician assistant, specializing in neurology, patient empowerment has always been an integral part of my care. Lori's story illustrated empowerment at the highest level. Watching her video peaked my interest as a climber and as a clinician.

I wondered what Lori was doing after completing the Seven Summits and learned from her website that she was organizing an expedition to Kilimanjaro with several individuals also diagnosed with MS. Kilimanjaro was on my bucket list, and I couldn't imagine a more amazing adventure than to trek Kilimanjaro with a team of people who had the courage to set a course that could redefine what it means to have a neurological disease. Although I didn't have MS, I was overwhelmed with emotion that maybe there was a slim chance I could become part of something that symbolized the very essence of how I care for my patients. I learned early in my career that empowerment is essential for people who live with a brain condition that slowly takes away their ability to walk, talk, and sometimes even their ability to think.

I have spent years working with a doctor who espouses empowerment at every chance by embracing patient-centered care and holistic treatments. Despite feeling I could be rejected or completely dismissed as a little bit crazy for wanting to invite some of my patients, I emailed Lori and asked if I and the doctor could join her team, and if yes, could I also invite a few of my patients with Parkinson's disease to come along? It was a long week as I waited for Lori to respond. During that time, I couldn't stop talking about Lori's heart-touching YouTube video and her amazing accomplishment in climbing the highest peak on each continent as she lived with MS. To my great surprise, Lori emailed me back and said yes. My world would be forever changed by this tiny mountaineer.

Many people posed the question, "You think people with Parkinson's can climb mountains?" This was a common question from my medical colleagues after learning I had signed up to climb Mt. Kilimanjaro. The surprise on their faces wasn't that I was heading off on another climb but that I planned to offer the opportunity to a few of my patients who have Parkinson's disease. I pondered their initial reaction and did start to question my decision, but only briefly.

Before offering the climb to anyone with Parkinson's disease, Dr. Giroux and I had long conversations about whether the risk was too great. We discussed the physical and mental challenges our patients would face on an alpine climb. Stress is known to worsen the symptoms of Parkinson's and MS until the stress is removed, and something as benign as the common cold can have serious consequences. Walking and muscle spasms can worsen and even cause movement to become impossible. We didn't know if medications would work well enough on the mountain or if the change in food would interfere with medication absorption. Nausea is a common medication side effect. It could potentially mimic altitude sickness that might complicate the triage process. Typical bladder problems associated with Parkinson's and MS could lead to infection.

Would we need additional antibiotics? Would our teammates with Parkinson's or MS be able to crawl out of their sleeping bag each morning or be immobilized from the confined space, a common symptom of Parkinson's? We had no answers for many of the concerns we discussed and agreed we would not stand in the way of anyone with Parkinson's disease who wanted to try. Although we agreed to proceed in putting the word out—that Lori had spots available on her team for a few people with Parkinson's— ultimately we would carry these worries with us until we returned.

The reaction to the adventure was even more surprising when I mentioned the climb to my patients. As they told their own stories of high adventure in days past, I noticed energy emanating from them that I had not seen before. Sadly, I was hearing their stories for the first time, and even more unsettling was the knowledge that all of the memories they shared about past adventures had taken place before their Parkinson's diagnoses. Although their adventurous hearts remained, the empowerment or belief that adventure was still possible for them had become missing in their lives.

I wondered, as medical practitioners, how much our perceptions of disease impacted the patients' perceptions of ability and disability. I quickly realized that for our patients to live their best lives, we must not only focus on their medical needs but also on their abilities. As medical providers, we have the power to encourage or discourage, and our words can empower or hold back our patients. I felt sure I had made the right decision to join a climbing team of individuals with MS and to open the door for people living with Parkinson's. This would be an opportunity to take part in empowering my patients and many others to take that next step and pursue the dream of a lifetime.

I was intrigued when many of my patients from all stages of disease wanted to go on the climb, affirming the power of community, the power of hope, and the possibility that the adventurous spirit could be restored. The open spots on the team quickly filled. The climb attracted individuals who had a wide range of experiences with strenuous physical activity and varied medical histories. A few individuals had dealt with Parkinson's for more than 10 years and one person even had a deep brain stimulator to control severe symptoms.

I signed on as a medical companion for the team, a substantial task in retrospect. The "what ifs" weighed heavily on my mind. Dr. Monique Giroux, our neurologist and companion climber, would provide insights into potential neurologic symptoms of MS and PD for the guides, and we would provide an environment of support for the whole team.

I had worked 12 years in a neurology specialty clinic and my previous climbing experience did ease my mind somewhat—I would not have to learn climbing skills but could focus on the health of the team. However, I would learn quickly that Mt. Kilimanjaro presented a very different challenge. Constant dust and increasing elevation would be an unknown stress on our team of 10 people with MS, 4 with PD, and 14 companions. This was not the typical climbing team. The following description of the days we spent on Mt. Kilimanjaro is reconstructed from my personal journal entries recorded at the end of each day.

On the mountain, our support for the climb was substantial. We set off that first day, July 13, 2011, with 2 American guides, 11 Tanzanian guides, and 136 porters. We left the Machame gate eager to begin the long trek. Walking steadily along the densely forested trail that weaved through the rainforest, the chatter of nervous energy flowed down the line. As we walked up the steep trail, my mind became preoccupied, wondering if I would be able to complete the climb. I had experienced severe altitude sickness on Mt. Rainier back in 2009 and knew how disabling it can be, striking at any time. What if I couldn't make it and then someone needed my help? My thoughts were soon distracted by listening to the life stories of my companions as we marched higher into the forest.

We carried a small backpack with the essentials, including rain gear, hats, sunblock, snacks and water, headlamps, warm layers, cameras, medications, and personal care items. We also brought waterproof boundary bags stuffed full of items we would use throughout the climb, such as sleeping bags and pads, bag liners, extra clothes, down jackets and pants, hats, gloves, batteries, more personal care items, and snacks. Our porters carried the boundary bags on their heads and shoulders, always reaching camp well before the team in order to set up the tents and prepare the meals.

Midway to our first camp, with the sun still high, we came upon a long dining table ready with lunch. What a surprise and delight that on this first day, and each subsequent one, we were served three full meals and could sit together to get to know each other more deeply. The meals became a special time of day for catching up with people we had not seen on the trail.

After lunch on Day One, the trail steepened and many reached camp after dark. The first day covered 5.4 miles to an elevation of 9,800 feet, an elevation gain of 4,160 feet in just over nine hours. Exhausted from hiking, I searched for my boundary bag and an empty tent to unpack sleeping gear, clean clothing, and toiletries. I was greeted by a porter with a basin of warm water and a drink. After quickly washing up, I put on warmer clothes and followed the sounds of my teammate's voices through the darkness to the dining tent. A hot dinner was waiting.

Eric, our lead guide, discussed what to expect the following day and addressed any concerns from the team. After dinner, I was called to triage an eye problem. The problem turned out to be an eye infection. I borrowed eye drops from the guide's first aid kit and applied a cleverly-made warm compress comprised of a hand warmer in a moist bandana. Then it was time to turn in for the night. Sleep came easy in a crisp 32 degrees. The team was doing well; we had passed through the jungle, and the mountain would be in view tomorrow.

We woke at 6:00 a.m. to repack the boundary bags and backpacks. Large containers of un-sanitized water from the mountain springs were carried by the porters so that we would have plenty on hand. We filled our empty water bottles and applied a chemical treatment to avoid dysentery. We added iodine sterilization tablets to the water in our bottles and then waited 30 minutes for the iodine to kill any bacteria or viruses. This process turned the water in our bottles an unappealing dingy yellow color. Thankfully, a neutralizing tablet was then added to eliminate the yellow color of the iodine.

Breakfast was as nutritious and tasty as dinner. We left camp around 9:00 a.m. after everyone had eaten and packed up their gear. The trek to Shira Camp took only about six hours for a 2,540 feet elevation gain to 12,500 feet. The trek to Shira included some rock scrambling and a nice addition to the sparse vegetation of the Moorlands. Altitude headaches were reported by several on the team when ascending above 11,000 feet, which then became the focus of conversation. I developed a crushing headache around 11,500 feet and started my usual medication cocktail for altitude headache, which included Diamox, ibuprofen and Tylenol.

Dinner was the time to check oxygen saturation levels and review how we were all feeling. I was relieved that everyone had moved well up the trail that day and managed the varied terrain without stumbles or falls. After a discussion about the symptoms and treatments for acute mountain sickness, Dr. Giroux and I remained close by as a teammate injected a medication for MS. We waited for 15 minutes to monitor whether they had an allergic reaction. No reaction was reported! We quickly crawled into our sleeping bags by 10:00 p.m. The night was clear with the mountain glowing under an almost full moon. The evening temperatures dropped to just below freezing that night.

My pounding altitude headache had been only slightly better after dinner and I lay awake wondering if the headache experienced by many on the team would improve without more aggressive medication management by the guides. The guides insisted everyone drink more water and breathe more often to reduce headaches. Although breathing deeper and more often can help reduce altitude headaches, our teammates with MS and Parkinson's did not necessarily have the extra energy reserves for the increased work of breathing. I worried the guides might not fully understand the complexity of symptoms our teammates had to deal with in addition to the crushing altitude headache. To avoid compromising the guides' authority, I had kept my opinions about treating altitude headaches to myself, at least at that point.

Knowing that we would be above the clouds for the next four days, the big question on many minds that night was what the next 7,000 feet and more than 20 miles would have in store for those with PD or MS. We could see how far away the summit ridge lay. Would muscles cramp and refuse to go another step? Would vision become so blurry that the trail would disappear from sight? Would nausea cause vomiting of critical medications? Would altitude sickness stand in the way of reaching our goal to finish what we had started? These questions were on our minds but did not stop anyone from moving forward. The 14 people facing PD and MS every step of the way displayed extraordinary courage. The 14 companions showed extraordinary kindheartedness and encouragement without being overbearing or overprotective.

Day Three was a repeat of Day Two but with a much longer day, hiking almost 10 hours from Shira Plateau to the Barranco Valley. We trekked into the alpine desert zone that had even less vegetation and many more lava rocks. Several on the team decided to climb to the base of Lava Tower at 15,500 feet. This was a good day for much needed acclimatization due to the ongoing headaches reported by the team. Since first arriving in Tanzania, one person on the team had a cough, which was getting worse by the day. I was concerned about the others catching what appeared to be a viral respiratory infection that could impact the health of the entire team. The six-mile trek on Day Three required more stops to rest cramping muscles, weak legs, sore feet, and achy joints. Going slow was also a way to reduce the impact of the thinning air at altitude that was causing headaches. We were fortunate to have a physical therapist on the team who was quick to massage cramping muscles. Occasionally a team member needed a break from carrying their backpack. However, suggesting that someone actually take that break required great finesse, as no one on the team was willing to do less.

Some of the companion climbers expressed growing concerns to Dr. Giroux and me about the muscle spasms and joint pain, noticeable in the teammates with MS and PD. We decided to stay close, go slow, and assist only if needed; we didn't want to draw a lot of attention to anyone's symptoms. We all knew the climb wasn't going to be a walk in the park and so we had to be comfortable seeing the symptoms when they appeared. Dr. Giroux and I talked confidently that if the symptoms got bad enough, we believed our teammates would ask for help.

We wanted to set the example to not act alarmed when symptoms became obvious. We needed to be supportive but not overbearing.

We also began checking oxygen levels more often due to the breathing problems of a few on the team. With normal oxygen saturation levels being 99-100%, everyone's oxygen saturation checks were holding steady between 77% and 95%. The consistency in oxygen saturation values for each person was a sign that the person was compensating for the altitude, but low oxygen saturation that was less than 80% required close monitoring. Dropping below 70% oxygen saturation would likely result in being placed on bottled oxygen and moved to a lower altitude or taken off the mountain. On the mountain at high altitude, oxygen saturation is expected to drop slowly with ascent and the body compensates by breathing deeper and more often. I had concerns that the respiratory virus in a couple of our teammates could turn an expected gradual change in oxygen status to a very serious medical condition.

Most of the team consumed five to six liters of water per day trying to ward off the unrelenting, pounding headaches associated with altitude that a growing number of people experienced. Thankfully, my headache started to improve after a couple days on Diamox. Had it not improved, going higher would have been difficult if not impossible. Each person on the team had their personal doctor prescribe Diamox and a few asked me what I thought about using it to treat their headaches. In each case, I said if they had a worsening headache that wasn't relieved by the guide's recommendations; then they should use their prescription and make sure to let the guide know.

Barranco Camp was our destination on Day Three. Located at 12,900 feet, it was only slightly higher in elevation than the night before. We arrived in camp at 5:30 p.m. and dinner was at 7:00 p.m.; there was no time to rest. Boundary bags had to be unpacked and tents readied for sleep. Self-care focused on treating headaches, sore feet, and sore muscles. Water treatment and personal hygiene were a priority and growing more and more time-consuming due to the diminishing oxygen in the atmosphere with each increase in elevation. The work of breathing tapped into vital energy stores needed to just move about the camp. At sea level, these evening tasks would not have been a problem but at almost 13,000 feet, our bodies just didn't move as fast. I could only imagine how the symptoms of Parkinson's or MS were taking a toll on precious energy reserves. At this point in the trek, yellow water from the iodine treatment was starting to look acceptable as we adjusted to life on the mountain and the absence of running water or hot showers. No one on the team complained nor did anyone ask to be treated differently. Most of the time, it wasn't obvious who had MS or PD; we were just one team moving together and supporting one another.

The first medical threat on the mountain happened on the third night. During dinner, a teammate reported chest pain. After Dr. Giroux and I spent hours of triage and close monitoring, the chest pain turned out to be a bad case of heartburn. A relief, but also a reality check that alpine trekking is a serious activity with serious risks.

After monitoring the nightly medication injections, Dr. Giroux and I rushed to the tent to settle and warm up. We needed some time alone to discuss the events of the day. The trek and altitude were wearing down some members of the team. We talked quietly about who we should stay close to the following day and reviewed some of the possible medical issues that might come up in the days to come. The team maintained a very positive attitude, and each day brought us closer together. During the night, however, someone was vomiting. The next morning as I packed up my boundary bag, I overheard people talking about how the altitude sickness was getting worse. Someone had begun to vomit and couldn't eat or drink. Neither Dr. Giroux nor I had been approached by the guides during the night to offer help so we assumed the guides had everything under control.

On Day Four, after Dr. Giroux and I triaged knee pain and a swollen eye, we prepared mentally for the steep rock wall that lie ahead between us and the next camp. The impact of altitude was obvious, with more coughing, headaches, nausea, and vomiting. However, no one was ready to go back to the hotel. By breakfast everyone was packed and ready to go. More weight was put in the boundary bags and less in the backpacks as we faced the 800-foot Barranco Wall. The wall was steep—some maneuvers required a big reach with little exposure. The wall was considered a scramble for some and ominous for others who had never rock climbed before.

The team was exhilarated after topping the wall. We could see the distant ridge where High Camp was located. The team moved along slowly across the Karanga Valley until we reached Karanga Camp. A few had slowed considerably and reached camp later in the afternoon. We caught up with our teammate who had been vomiting in the night. She was sitting by the trail with our lead guide. She still had not been able to eat any food or drink much water and her green-tinged skin was more than a little concerning. The guide said he would keep an eye on her and waved us on. Reluctantly we moved on; camp was just a mile or so away.

This was our last afternoon to catch up on some rest. Karanga Camp was a three-mile trek and would provide another day for acclimatization. We slept at 13,000 feet, a minimal increase in elevation. The headaches, nausea, and coughing continued and seemed to be worse on that day. Loose stools became a normal topic of conversation. Although everyone had Diamox, it was not being consistently used for altitude symptoms. Our guide insisted we use breathing techniques, hydration, ibuprofen, and acetaminophen to offset the low partial pressure of oxygen in the air. The use of Diamox was decided on a case-by-case basis, and more of the team began to use their prescriptions.

Like the art of medicine, there is an art to managing a team that is experiencing the altitude effects of an alpine environment. Despite popular opinion, there seemed to be ongoing debate in the guiding community over whether to use Diamox for altitude symptoms. Its use can cause dehydration, dizziness, and tingling of the skin, all of which could be confused with a neurologic problem. At high doses, Diamox can even decrease physical performance. Using Diamox when guiding individuals with neurological conditions has pros and cons and each holds valid concern. We understood that Diamox can and should be used conservatively if alternative strategies are not effective against an unrelenting headache. The team remained concerned about the persistent headaches and nausea that were affecting most on the team. To make matters even more stressful, we learned over dinner that we would be at High Camp the following day and would actually head for the summit before midnight. This was our last night to get sleep before the summit.

Day Five didn't start out too well. The coughing and oxygen saturation were worse among a few and headaches and nausea persisted. During the night, one person had developed severe sinus pain and a few others began to show more symptoms of a respiratory infection. After triaging the sinus pain, fever, and chills, we headed out for the three-mile trek to Barafu Camp located at 15,100 feet, where we had lunch. The daily temperature hovered around 68 degrees. Looking out, it seemed as if we would be able to walk across the dense cloud layer to the horizon. The cloud layer was contiguous with the edge of the mountain and stretched unbroken across the sky to the horizon. This gray bottomless, yet inviting, substance appeared solid, lacking the menacing dust that seemed to find any opening under the cloth that covered our noses and mouths.

The trail dust remained our biggest nuisance and threat to those with a cough. After lunch, we headed up to High Camp, named Kosovo—situated at 15,600 feet. We unpacked our boundary bags, prepared our gear for summit night, and added iodine treatments to several liters of water that we would need for the climb to the summit. Loss of appetite and diarrhea were reported by several members of the team. Everyone was tired but excited about going for the summit in only a few hours. We planned to leave in small groups starting at 10:45 p.m.; the team having been split into fast-, medium-, and slow-paced groups.

After an uneasy morning, everyone had made it to High Camp and enjoyed a final meal together before returning to our tents to rest for a few hours. We had trekked 23 miles so far. As each mile became a memory, so too did the labels of PD and MS. We were all one team, sharing one common goal and supporting each other in the biggest challenge of our lives.

Summit night was lit up under a full moon. The air was cold. We all wore our puffy down-filled jackets to keep warm. We had four miles to go—straight up to reach the summit. There wasn't much talking as everyone was kept busy with last-minute checks to make sure all our gear was packed. Another meal was waiting for us before we headed out. Although additional food was a good idea, nervous energy and altitude killed the appetite for many. I had lost my appetite the day before and only managed a few bites at each meal. Food had lost a lot of its appeal.

We could see a string of headlamps from other teams that had gotten an earlier start. The lights dotted the path to Stella's Point, the resting place before making the long march along the crater rim to the summit. The effects of altitude took a great toll on some team members who were experiencing worsening respiratory problems and symptoms of altitude sickness. Some had to turn back after reaching 17,000 feet and struggling to take a breath or walk another step. The need and decision for some to turn back was an emotional pain that seemed to far outweigh any physical discomfort they felt as a result of the trek or medical condition.

Each group moved at a varied pace and even the groups ended up further divided with each person setting their own tempo. There were a lot of worries about what was happening below as stories that some were not doing well trickled up the line of the slow-moving climbers. Water and food froze in the cold night and my ability to move along the switchbacks and climb over large boulders was too slow to generate body heat to stay warm. My muscles started to shiver and stiffen as each breath inhaled cold air that chilled my core. I put on all my warm clothing layers, took some ibuprofen and Tylenol and continued the march to the summit. I wondered how my teammates were doing above and below.

We all suffered from the effects of altitude, but some on the team endured much more in their quest to reach the summit, with muscles under the control of MS or Parkinson's. I had many thoughts of turning around when my breathing could not keep up with the oxygen demands of my muscles and each cold breath felt like a knife edging into my lung. Frequently needing to rest, I sat on any flat-topped boulder that my rational mind knew would steal precious body heat from me. *If only the sun would appear,* I thought, *I will finally feel warm and safe from the dark and cold mountain.* With each pause at yet another boulder, I heard Dr. Giroux, who was but one step behind, say firmly, "Keep moving, we are almost there."

Once reaching Stella's Point at over 18,000 feet, the sun was just breaking through the distant horizon. With each step moving me closer to the summit, I could feel the growing warmth of the sun and I knew that I would soon reach it. I could see a crowd of people in the distance. *That must be the summit*, I thought. All doubt left and I was renewed with confidence. I knew I would make it. With only a quarter mile to go, I felt like running but I knew I had to go slow or risk getting sick. As I passed the glaciers of Kilimanjaro, I felt exhilarated. I took out my camera and shot as many pictures as possible to preserve the memories forever. In all my dreams of climbing, I had never imagined that I would feel so energized at 19,000 feet.

The temperature on the summit was 17 degrees. We were blessed with very little wind and clear skies. Reaching the 19,340-foot summit was a humbling experience filled with an overflow of emotion that was enhanced by the camaraderie amongst the team. I did not feel invincible or special. I felt lucky that the mountain had provided a good night in which to climb and that my mind had not given in to the constant ache for oxygen. I felt grateful that I had not turned around.

We stood patiently in line to take a group photo in front of the summit marker. The feeling on the summit with people with MS and Parkinson's was surreal. I knew we would have the summit photo to prove that we had been there and that, yes, people with Parkinson's and MS can climb a mountain. Seeing firsthand what the power of the mind can accomplish in pushing our physical limits brought flowing tears of joy and euphoria as I witnessed my teammates with MS and PD take those final slow and deliberate steps toward the summit. The feeling of compassion was simply overwhelming.

Most of the team reached the summit as the sun rose above the horizon. Dr. Giroux and I stayed on the summit for about 30 minutes, taking photos of the snowfields and glaciers and congratulating our teammates. I was surprised that I did not feel the effects of the altitude after the long night of pushing my body beyond its limits. I think the emotional side of my brain took over; leaving no awareness of the fatigue or dehydration that would soon become troublesome on the way down.

After the nine-hour ascent, we quickly descended down the loose scree, passing more teammates on their way to the summit. We were halfway into Day Six. We had to rest, rehydrate, and pack for the descent to Low Camp. Our exit, Mweka gate, was eight miles from High Camp. We were all utterly exhausted but determined to finish what we had started. One person was evacuated to Mweka gate on a man-powered stretcher due to spasticity, a condition of the muscles causing severe overactive contractions that can forcefully pull a joint in the wrong direction and result in pain and leg dragging. Another person had a bout of asthma that required short-term use of oxygen and an inhaler to open oxygen deprived airways. No serious medical problems emerged on the trek but we were all dehydrated and in need of a good night's sleep.

After a final night on the mountain, all but one walked out under their own power. The team had just accomplished the challenge of a lifetime.

My perspective has not changed since returning from Africa. Supporting a life of adventure for people living with neurological conditions empowers our patients to live life to the fullest. It is a responsibility we all share as medical providers and as a community to empower and instill hope so that precious victories are noticed and celebrated.

However, what has changed is my belief in the power of the mind and how critical positivity can be for people living with MS or Parkinson's. You see, they can climb rock walls, walk several miles a day, navigate varied terrain, acclimatize to altitude, sleep in tents, eat and drink in a dark dusty dining tent, attend to their own personal self-care, offer support to others, and be a part of an exciting adventure.

Since returning from Africa, my colleagues asked, "How did it go?" Their interest was more about what happened each day on the mountain and not who made the summit. I replied to the question with unquestionable resolve that the Leap of Faith Kilimanjaro climb was an adventure that changed the perception of what it means to have a neurological disease. It takes courage to climb a high mountain; much like the courage our patients must have to get out of bed each morning to face yet another day with a disease. I continue to speak in front of groups to tell our story with hopes of empowering the audience to believe anything is possible when we tap into the positive power of the mind and leave behind the fears and labels of living with a neurologic disease.

I owe great appreciation to Lori Schneider, our inspirational team leader and mentor, for setting an example of courage and strength that has redefined the possibilities for people with neurological conditions and changed the perception of disability in the medical community. The Kilimanjaro adventure set in motion a change in both Dr. Giroux and me that led to a new beginning and a new adventure.

With newfound courage and strength, we decided to follow our passion to offer patient-centered care in a holistic and wellness environment and leave our regimented institutional jobs behind. We moved to Denver, Colorado to start anew and opened our own clinic where we are no longer restricted from developing programs to empower our patients—a place where thinking outside the box is part of the normal routine. The name of the new clinic, "Movement and Neuroperformance Center," fits with our focus on abilities and wellness instead of disease and disabilities. Whether destiny or just plain luck, Dr. Giroux and I have taken a great leap of faith in believing we can make a difference in the lives of our patients.

Sierra Farris is a physician assistant specialized in neurologic conditions and deep brain stimulation. Sierra is co-owner of the Movement & Neuroperformance Center Colorado located in Denver (www.centerformovement.org), a medical clinic that offers patient centered and holistic care. Her passion for climbing peaks and patient empowerment opened the door to an amazing adventure to Africa's Mt. Kilimanjaro. Sierra and her climbing companion, Dr. Monique Giroux, offered their support so patients with Parkinson's could take the challenge of a lifetime and climb a mountain. Sierra is an author, researcher, bioethicist, clinician and mountaineer. In combining her compassion and enthusiasm for reaching beyond self-imposed limits, Sierra inspires her patients to live life to the fullest by focusing on one's abilities, not disabilities.

A Person Worth Fighting For

Gina Anderson

CHANGE HAPPENS SO SLOWLY. SOMETIMES YOU don't even realize you've changed.

In 2003, I was diagnosed with macular dystrophy. At the time, I was not too concerned. As a band director, I felt I could do my job with or without my central vision. One day, however, I overheard a conversation between my principal and two other teachers. They were making fun of a parent who had a vision impairment. I felt very hurt and wondered how long it would be before they began to make fun of me.

I had always chosen to be a part of the best schools in music education, but I quickly learned that they often chose and judged staff based on the way they looked rather than on their education, experience, and achievements. In the past, I would have been the one standing up for the underdog—in this case on behalf of the parent. I would have blurted out that what they were doing was wrong or I would have sent a letter stating their wrongdoing in writing. That night I wrote a letter to my principal, but I never sent it. Instead, after that incident, I started to distance myself from my co-workers and the internal politics, and I became increasingly dissatisfied with me. I began to withdraw and change, yet I didn't even realize what was happening. It was as if I became ashamed of myself and wanted to hide.

During college, I took a class about students with special needs. I remembered the professor telling us that we needed to teach the students what to do when they came home from their jobs. This advice struck a chord with me. Now, it became relevant to my life, too. What would I do? How would I care for me?

I realized I had to find sports activities I could do without my sight. In the past, I'd enjoyed sports that had a ball involved, but I knew I wouldn't be able to play those anymore. I considered golf but understood I'd always have to have someone along to help me. I wanted to find a sport I could do on my own. I even thought about bike riding on familiar roads. Without my sight, I believed I could use my side vision to guide the bike on roads I knew well. As I looked at my options, I considered how I don't like waiting for anyone—I didn't want to *have to* wait for others so I could go for a workout. I like to do things when I'm in the mood, no matter the time of day. I also thought about my need to be independent. Once I couldn't do my job, I would need to fill my days with independent activities while others were at work. Otherwise, I'd go nuts!

What started as an exploration of things I could do when I got home from work, and continue to do later in life, turned into a great enjoyment of triathlons. I started to read and learn as much as I could about the sport and began to compete. I set a goal of doing an Ironman Distance triathlon. I thought I could do one with sight and eventually one without sight. This became my focus for the next few years.

The year 2009 was a very difficult one for my family. My brother was in a deep depression and lost his home. I had a severe allergic reaction to an antibiotic that turned into Steven-Johnson Syndrome, a potentially deadly skin disease caused by a drug reaction. My dad was diagnosed with hairy cell leukemia. We also lost three other close family members. In spite of all of these difficulties, I decided to do my first Ironman triathlon. The training increased so that by summer I was doing 11 very long workouts each week. They seemed to become a full-time job!

On the day my dad was being released from the hospital, after his initial diagnosis and first chemo treatment, I experienced strange vision on my right side. I had planned a training ride on my bike that day and was wearing wraparound glasses. Sometimes it takes a few minutes to get used to them and I thought I just needed time to adjust. After riding for some time I noticed that the vision problem was not going away. For such a basic training day, I also felt unusually tired. When I arrived home, I carried my bike upstairs to its room—yes, my bike has its own room. Walking up the stairs, my legs felt like lead weights. I thought that my legs were filled with lactic acid. Since I'd been experiencing these symptoms for some time, I attributed how I was feeling to my arduous training schedule.

The next day, when I was out in the backyard with my dogs, I also noticed that the trees looked funny. Something was definitely wrong, but I couldn't quite figure out what. I didn't want to mention it to my family because they had enough to worry about with my dad's health issues. So I drove into town and did my swim training of 5,000 yards, all the while knowing that something was off. I felt okay at the swim workout, but in the afternoon when I went for my run, I had a lot of trouble getting back to my house. I was exhausted!

By the next morning I knew that my eyesight was getting worse and that I needed to see my optometrist soon, so I made the appointment. That night as I lay in bed, I started to cry. I felt certain that this would be my last night as a sighted person. On the following day, I expected to get the news that the macular dystrophy was progressing rapidly.

My optometrist knew by the look on my face that something was wrong. She examined my eyes and said they looked normal, or as normal as my eyes could look. What was happening was not from the macular dystrophy, she assured me. She recommended I see my primary care doctor. I left the appointment feeling good and thinking that whatever was going on, it was something that could be fixed. While I was doing dishes that night, however, I looked out the window toward the curb across the street and saw one curb on top of the other—I had double vision, another new development.

The next day I went to see my primary care physician. I saw a very intelligent third-year medical student. Because of the information I had given over the phone, they arranged for another doctor to observe the exam. At the time I only thought it was my eyesight that was the problem—and the focus of their exam. The simple neurological test she gave me did not show anything unusual, because I was extremely strong from training for the triathlon. The Ironman was only five weeks away and I kept asking if we could fix "this" so I would be able to participate.

It was a long appointment, as the doctors discussed what to do next. They ordered an MRI, which was set to take place within two days. I noticed that they had written multiple sclerosis as a possible diagnosis on the MRI form. However, not knowing anything about MS at the time, I didn't feel overly concerned. Because there are few neurologists where I live, it actually took two weeks before I was seen.

By the following day my eyesight had become much worse and I knew I should not be driving. For the next two weeks my brother stepped up and drove me around. He was living on one side of a duplex that we had purchased together. Little did we know when we made this move that it would turn out to be the answer to what followed. My mom was busy with my dad and my brother was able to take care of me.

My eyesight turned out to not be the only problem I began to notice. One day, as I held my 27-pound dog and talked to the dog groomer, I had difficulty holding her in my arms. They felt so fatigued that I thought I would drop her. When I did put her down, my arms trembled. These symptoms continued as I waited through the weeks until my doctor's appointment.

When I filled out the paperwork at the neurologist's office, I could tell that something else wasn't right. The pen I was using did not feel *right* in my hand. I casually mentioned this to the doctor when I saw him. He became excited and asked me to write some things down. He told me to write all of the different activities that I do: swimming, biking, skiing, and running. Then he asked me, "Is this your handwriting?" I said, "No, this is a lot sloppier than I normally write." Although my handwriting isn't normally neat, this was a lot worse.

He then sat back in his chair and said, "I know what this says, but it is difficult for me to tell you." I was thinking that even though he had a thick accent, I could understand him quite clearly. *Why was this so difficult to tell me?* It turned out what he actually meant was how difficult it would be to tell me, an active person, that I had a disease that could impede my activity levels. He was already thinking about what the future might hold for me. As I sat there, he started to explain multiple sclerosis.

He said I would need to go into the hospital on Tuesday for steroid treatments. It was Friday, so I was allowed to go home for three days and get things in order. He also told me that he believed I'd be okay for those three days; I didn't know what he meant by that. When I went out to the car, I told my brother very matter-of-factly that I had multiple sclerosis and needed to go into the hospital the following Tuesday for about five days. My exact words were, "Well, I guess I have multiple sclerosis." He looked back at me with more shock than I felt.

The doctor sent me home with a folder full of information to read through before I went into the hospital the following week. Since I still didn't understand much about MS, all I could think about that weekend was the impending spinal tap—I knew how painful they are and wasn't looking forward to having one.

I was so busy that weekend preparing for my hospital stay and calling around to find a substitute teacher who would cover our first week back to school, that it still hadn't hit me I had multiple sclerosis. As the three days progressed, I became quite weak. I remember sitting on the floor to get my Bach CDs out of the CD player. When I finally got them out, I tried to stand up and found that only one small muscle in my knee was firing on one side. I could feel that muscle stretching and stretching and realized it would soon tear if I kept going. It was working to its full strength while all the other muscles couldn't do anything. I sat back down on the floor and had to stay there for quite some time before my legs were ready to lift me up.

A leaden feeling of heaviness washed through my body as I lay in bed that night. I thought my breathing would stop if I didn't concentrate on it. That was the first time I became truly scared about having MS. I had this sense that if I went to sleep I would never wake up.

On Tuesday we were able to park close to the entrance of the hospital. All we had to do was walk across a skywalk, then take an elevator up to my floor. My room was right around the corner. By the time I reached it, I was weak and tired and felt that leaden sensation throughout my entire body. I sat in the chair in my room, unable to do anything for a few hours.

I never left my room while I was in the hospital and didn't want to see anybody. I was to be released on Saturday. The Ironman race for which I'd trained so hard would take place that Sunday, and I was extremely angry about not being able to do it. My arms were so weak I even had difficulty opening pepper packets made out of paper. I couldn't believe how strong I had been just a few weeks earlier and couldn't understand how I had lost it all so fast. I didn't do anything during my hospital stay except listen to my Bach CDs.

One evening a few days after being released from the hospital, I decided to watch the Wisconsin news because it came on earlier than our local news. Just before the commercial break they announced that they would be talking to a woman with a neurological disorder—a woman who had just climbed Mount Everest. I thought, *What are the chances she has multiple sclerosis?* As tired as I was, I waited for the segment to air. Then they said the magic words, that Lori did have multiple sclerosis. As I watched the segment, I wrote down her name. When they asked her what she was going to do next, she talked about taking a group of people who had MS up Kilimanjaro.

I had never thought about climbing a mountain, but this seemed interesting to me. The challenge it presented came at a time when I needed one the most. I had tried to go back to work for two days each week but realized it was too soon. Halfway through the day, I'd get tired and become wobbly. So being homebound, I needed something to look forward to—something to focus on besides being sick.

That night I spent some time researching and reading the information on her website. Throughout the year, I continued to follow her on Facebook and through her website. The idea of climbing Kilimanjaro started to take root. I began to talk about the possibility with my students and asked what they thought about it. I downloaded all three seasons of Everest off of iTunes and started to watch them over and over. It was June 28, 2010 when I gathered the courage to contact Lori and ask her if she was still planning to do the trip. It only took her two hours to respond with her kind words of encouragement and information about the trip. The trip was moving forward and set for July of 2011.

To miss the Ironman triathlon after months of training had been devastating. After learning I had multiple sclerosis, I didn't feel that being in shape mattered much anymore. It seemed pointless to train for any kind of race, never knowing when I might relapse. It would be just another major disappointment if I didn't make it to the starting line. The hope and dream of doing this climb changed all of that. I continued to talk to people about the possibility of taking on this adventure and I slowly started to get back in shape. I began to enjoy the activities again, too. Thinking about this climb kept me moving during the summer of 2010.

Yet, when it came time to make the deposit to secure a place on the team, I doubted my ability to take this on. It took some trusted friends to push me off the fence and into this trip. Knowing that I had their support, as well as my family's, made me believe I could see this through. The trip was all I talked about the weekend of our family reunion.

The following week I received a call from the superintendent's office. My job had been cut back for the 2010-2011 school year; I was no longer a full-time teacher. Here I was committed to a great adventure, but facing financial uncertainty. I wondered whether I should pull out of the trip. Through Lori's encouragement, I decided to stick it out and work the hardest I have ever worked for a goal.

To keep my expenses down that year, I committed to training with what I had available to me at home and in the Upper Peninsula of Michigan. On the short days of winter I walked to the largest hill by my house, which is alongside a main road. I walked up and down it for two hours at a time, with a backpack full of my hand weights. As I found myself getting stronger, I needed a bigger hill, so I started to climb Mt. Marquette. I climbed up one side and down the other. I met other people out walking but I was the only one with serious hiking boots and what looked like a fully-loaded backpack.

By December, Lori had matched us with a companion climber, and we began to get to know each other. Suz and I fit together perfectly; she was very athletic and full of energy. She was just what I needed. Suz had also suffered a lot of hardship in her life and planned to share it with me on the mountain. I had never thought of my life as being difficult until I turned 40 and had to face so many challenges in such a short amount of time. Suz taught me that persevering after such hardships shapes you into one of the stronger people of the world.

It wasn't long after meeting Suz that my dad became very ill again. Between Christmas and over New Year's he was in intensive care fighting for his life. It was another hardship my family had to endure. One long day in the waiting area, working on puzzle number nine or so, my nephew, who looked at the positive side of things, said that this was family bonding time. Yep, another event meant to bring us together. My dad made it through the most difficult fight of his life and continued to fight through some setbacks over the next few months.

In the meantime, Suz had an idea to write a song to help raise money for my trip. Since Suz and I were both into music, it was a great idea. I contacted a friend of mine who composes music. Although he typically writes in a more classical style, he agreed to give "pop" a try. I sent him information about Lori's website to get ideas and inspiration for the piece. The words would be the most difficult, so I contacted my best friend, Josie Baughman, to see what she could come up with. She came up with the following poem:

On the continent of Africa
stands a white, shining peak.
Mount Kilimanjaro
is not for the meek.

It is not the mountain we conquer,
when we reach the summit.
But ourselves through a Leap of Faith,
when we climb beyond our self-imposed limit.

It is More than a Mountain,
it is more than a quest.
Empowered through adventure,
we give our very best.

Brandon liked the poem so much that he decided to use it in its entirety. The project was coming together very nicely. When Suz, a singer, got the music in her hands, she went to work recording it. I thought there should be something else on the CD. Being a trumpet player, I looked for trumpet music I could put on the CD. I found a Libby Larson piece that was written for a solo trumpet, called, "Fanfare for the Women." I contacted Libby Larson's publicist and told them about the project and the group. They liked the idea and directed me through the proper channels to get permission to use the work. Once I had the music in my hands I had about two days to learn the piece and record it. I have been teaching music for 16 years but had never done a project like this before. I found it to be a great experience—it felt good to focus on something other than all the training.

Over the next few months, Suz and I promoted the CD and kept up with our training. During this time, I had trouble with my hip and the back part of my leg. I could only hike two hours before my gait changed and it became very painful to walk. After all that my family and I had been through in the past year and a half, I really didn't want to go to the doctor, but I knew I needed to find out what was happening. A rush of anxiety washed over me as I thought about another doctor's appointment.

My doctor set me up with a great physical therapist who was also a hiker. It was refreshing; he didn't try to dissuade me from training. He just said to work up to the point that it became uncomfortable. After a few weeks of working with him, we discovered that I simply needed to stretch after a hike or workout. During our time together, he became interested in the trip. He even called me as I was driving home from the airport after the trip. I've told my students that every time you have contact with another person you touch their life. This seemingly small contact with him had a significant impact on me and has changed the way I think about healthcare—some people in the field truly do care about your wellbeing.

As the time was getting closer to the trip I began to have doubts. *Had I done enough training? Could I stay healthy and make it to the start? Did I have everything I needed? Would my family be okay and remain healthy while I was away?* Through Lori's emails I could tell that other people were having similar doubts. Lori's kind and reassuring words kept me going. I was determined to not only make it to the start of this climb, but also to the finish.

The day before we were to fly out of the U.S., Suz and I met at the home of another one of the companion climbers, Tina. The three of us had an instant bond. We decided to go for a walk that night because we were going to be sitting for endless hours over the next two days. It was on this walk that Suz talked about her personal story of tragedy for the first time. I knew then that I was in great hands with Suz as my partner—that I could tell her anything and she would be strong enough to handle it.

I also decided to leave all my problems and worries at home in Michigan while on this great adventure. I wanted to live in this moment. It was freeing to feel so unburdened; it was the greatest gift I could give myself. I was inspired by the new people around me, and I felt immediately at ease to be myself. There was no concern for what others might think about me or whether they were judging me. I knew we were all in this together.

The people of Tanzania do not own much; they work

extremely hard for the little money that they earn. Porters carry heavy loads up and down Mount Kilimanjaro every day, yet they seem very happy. Guides take your pack for you when you need help and sing all the while they are working. The joy expressed by the Tanzanians lifted my spirits daily. I realized there was a lot to learn from them. It is not possessions that make us happy, but all the little things we take for granted.

It was one such small thing that really motivated me to crawl out of my warm sleeping bag on cold mornings. Each day, a porter came to our tents to wake us. He brought hot water for coffee, tea, chocolate, or milk. This little luxury got me going each day—it was something I looked forward to every morning.

The experience of climbing the mountain and reaching the summit was exhilarating. The pictures do remind me of the trip and the astounding sights. As someone who is going to lose her sight, I find myself looking at the photos every day, trying to etch them into my mind. I want to remember the sounds, too—the shuffle of our feet on the path, the voices of the porters and guides talking in Swahili, the rocks falling from the western breach, and the sound of my breathing while I wore earplugs. These are just a few of the sounds I hear in my memories. The sights, sounds, and feelings of the time I spent in Tanzania will live with me always.

Change happens so slowly that you don't even realize you've changed until one day on a mountain you are given insight into your transformation. As I process this trip, my understanding of what is most important in life becomes stronger and clearer. This journey has changed me, and I know that my future path is up to me. It is difficult to plan for the future when you live with MS. Neither I nor my doctors can predict when the next relapse will occur or how severe it will be. Two years ago, Tyler Yelle, a student of mine, gave me a strip of paper with the following words written on it:

"Yesterday is old news and tomorrow never comes. Don't waste the time you have left in your today to dwell on the past or worry about tomorrow. Live in the now."

This may seem very insightful for such a young man, but Tyler understands the importance of living in the moment, as his father suffers from an inoperable brain tumor. Learning to live in the moment is not easy. It is something I must remind myself to do every single day, but the experience and accomplishment of summiting Mount Kilimanjaro serves as a wonderful reminder.

Before our trip, my climbing partner Suz gave me a gift. It was a necklace with the inscription: "I can, I will, I am – Kili 2011." This is what she says when facing a difficult situation. My path has been rocky, and I'm sure there will be other obstacles thrown in my way, but I know…**I *can* stand up for myself, I *will* stand up for myself, and I *am* a person worth fighting for.** And so are you!

***Gina Anderson** has taught in Washington, Wisconsin, and is currently a teacher in the Upper Peninsula of Michigan. She attended Baldwin-Wallace Conservatory of Music and the American Band College where she received her master's degree in conducting. She continues to be active with cross-country skiing, biking, running, swimming, hiking, ice climbing, igloo building and anything else that* *looks like fun, even if it gives her parents more gray hair. Her parents, Virgil and Sandy Anderson, will celebrate their 50th wedding anniversary in 2013, and as a family they are looking forward to a positive year. Ironman Wisconsin is in Gina's sight for 2014. Gina can be contacted at oboe906@ yahoo.com.*

The Giver Receives

"For it is in giving that we receive."
- Saint Francis of Assisi

Gaining Perspective

Daniel Wilkins

WHEN THE OPPORTUNITY TO PARTICIPATE IN THIS climb presented itself, I thought to myself: *This is the thing bigger than me that will finally put it all into perspective— what my life means and what I am supposed to do with it. It will wash away the years of pain and suffering. I will get the clarity I need to sober up.*

On my way to Tanzania, during a layover in Amsterdam, I began to write in my journal. I started the journal by writing that this trip meant freedom from everything that kept me shackled. I am not sure I knew exactly what those things were at the time, but reflecting back more than a year later, I can see that I was shackled by addiction, depression, and most of all fear. Although I was not consciously aware of it, my life had become almost completely driven by my fears.

In March, 2011, I accepted the invitation to join the group. It's amazing how life works. One of the participants reached out to me to see if my foundation, the Wilkins Parkinson's Foundation—co-founded with my father Bill after he was diagnosed with Parkinson's—could fund a documentary about the trip. I told her we didn't do that type of work, however, I was personally interested in going. Doing a climb had been on my list of things I wanted to accomplish in my life, and this was the perfect time to do it, before my wife and I welcomed a child into our lives. After an "interview" with Lori, she called me a couple of days later to say she thought I would be a great fit for one of the climbers who had PD, Nathan.

The climb was scheduled for July, giving me three months to train for a 19,340-foot mountain climb, quite an undertaking when I live in Atlanta at an altitude of about 1,000 feet. I had no prior experience with this type of adventure.

The truth is, although I wanted to do this climb and knew this was an incredible opportunity on so many levels, I wasn't excited about spending two weeks with people I didn't know. I wasn't thrilled in the least about sharing a tent for a week on the side of a mountain with someone I didn't know beyond a few back-and-forth email conversations. Quite honestly, I was so consumed with what was going on for me and so far into the isolation fueled by depression and addiction that I almost backed out of the trip.

I knew deep down, though, that this climb had the potential to change me. Somewhere inside myself, I knew I had to do something. In my twisted mind, this climb sounded easier than admitting to another human being that I had a problem, that I probably needed help, and that I might need to enter rehab. I still felt like I could beat this on my own. From my distorted viewpoint, all I needed was a spiritual experience to help put everything into perspective. Selfishly, that's how I approached this trip. Not to help my climbing partner or the other climbers. Not to raise awareness for Parkinson's disease. I pushed myself to join this climb for *my* problems and *my* issues.

By the time I arrived in Tanzania I felt extremely rundown. On top of the jet lag, I missed my wife Kristin tremendously. It isn't typical for me to be overly emotional about missing people, but because I knew our contact would be limited for the impending two weeks, I felt anxious and alone.

Everyone going on the climb went through gear check, orientation, and more orientation. During the first days in Arusha, our group never made it out into the city, which was disappointing to me. It certainly didn't help to keep my mind off my wife, my life, and not drinking.

What did help was getting to know my climbing partner and roommate Nathan. Nathan's strength of character showed through very early on, and it helped me keep focused on the task at hand. Looking back on it now, Nathan played a tremendous role in my reaching the summit. However, even with the welcomed distraction of getting to know Nathan, I was not excited about the climb. Instead, I was filled with anxiety about not being able to summit and the very real possibility of letting him down. This anxiety, on top of the whirlwind of emotions I was feeling even before departing for Africa, made for a frustrating and tough first few days.

Once we finally made it into the Kilimanjaro National Park, with the beauty of the mountain and scenery around me, I finally started to relax. I wasn't thinking about drinking as much or about my problems. I began to focus more on Nathan—on making sure I knew as much about his specific PD symptoms and learning what I could do to help along the way. He wrote down his medications, dosages, and administration times for me. I set reminders to ensure he didn't forget to take his meds. We continued to get to know one another and I was starting to feel more comfortable with the friendships I was developing with other people in our group as well.

Once we started the hike it finally felt as though the rest of the world didn't matter. The only thing that counted was the task directly in front of us. The first day's hike through the rainforest was tough and steep. Nathan and I were in the first group to reach our stopping point for the evening. It took us about six hours to hike to Camp 1.

Day Two of hiking was relatively uneventful but filled with beautiful scenery. The best part for me was getting to Camp 2 and having the opportunity to sit down and get to know Nathan, John, and Martha better. I felt the most comfortable with them and I enjoyed their company. The landscape around Camp 2 was unbelievable too. We were above the clouds at an elevation of about 12,500 feet. This was the highest I had ever been, but the altitude didn't seem to bother me too much. We witnessed a breathtaking sunset unlike any I had ever seen before. The colors were so vivid that as the clouds blew in, a colorful, misting-like affect was created through the various outcroppings of the adjacent mountains. I recall asking our lead guide, Eric, how this particular sunset matched up to others he had seen on the mountain. He told me it was one of the best, if not the best, he had ever seen, and that we were very lucky to be watching it.

I slept well that night, given how exhausting the hike had been. I woke up freezing in the middle of the night, despite the fact that I was wearing four layers on top, two on bottom, two pairs of wool socks, and a beanie cap on my head. Worse than the cold, I awoke with the most intense headache I have ever experienced. The altitude had finally gotten to me. I panicked because we had been basing altitude sickness symptoms on a scale of 1-5 and this felt like a 50! I was scared this would be the end of the road for me and that I would let Nathan down. I suffered through the headache until morning, then chugged a liter of water and took some Advil as I focused on some specific breathing techniques. After about 30 minutes, the symptoms subsided to a tolerable level, and by the time I finished with breakfast I was back to 95%.

The day that followed was long. It took us about eight hours to reach our next camp. A few of us took a small detour to a higher elevation to see the Lava Fields and to further acclimate to the altitude. I took the opportunity to check out what one of the outhouses along the trail looked like on the inside. All I can say, without getting too descriptive, is that we were a very fortunate group to have the toilet tents that our porters carried for us.

By the time we got into camp that evening, we were absolutely wiped out. The last three hours or so had been downhill as we hiked to lower altitude to sleep for the night. Nathan's meds seemed to be wearing off a little bit and he had some trouble with his footing on a couple of occasions. Our guide and I were able to catch him, and no one got hurt, but it definitely added to the difficulty of the day. Nathan seemed a little embarrassed; however, I told him that it was no problem at all. I was sure he would have his chance to grab me before the trip was over.

What Nathan didn't know was that he helped me every day by trudging on and never complaining. He showed me more strength than I had seen in another single individual in a long time. Every evening as I watched Nathan and the other climbers come into camp after hiking all day, I was moved to tears. Everyday these folks overcame fears and obstacles, half of them doing it while battling MS or Parkinson's disease. Here I was wrapped up in my own bullshit and these people were showing so much courage— courage I could only wish to possess someday. I finished out the day performing minor surgery on an ingrown hair on the side of my face and attending to athlete's foot that had gotten so bad I thought my foot might rot off before I reached the summit.

That evening the journalist who was accompanying the trip (Jeff) shared a poem he had written about the sound, or song, that a landscape makes if you listen carefully enough to it. After he read his poem I went outside to reflect on his words. I sat on a rock overlooking the clouds below us and the blinding light of the stars above us. Although I have a difficult time now recalling the melody I heard that evening, I did write in my journal that I thought I could hear the mountain's song to us.

The next day's climb started up what was almost a vertical rock face. This was the first time we encountered what required hand-over-hand climbing up the trail. To this point, if someone had fallen, the worst that would have happened was a broken bone or two. If any of us had fallen off the face, however, we surely would have died and might have taken a few people along with us. This was the only time I was really concerned about Nathan's ability to get to the next camp. If he had slipped like he'd done the previous day, there would have been no chance for me to catch him. My fears were for nothing—Nathan did amazingly well. We made it to camp without any problems, which was at 13,200 feet.

At this point in the trip, I made a note in my journal that despite the fact my personality defects kept me from developing any deep connections with the majority of the group, what they had accomplished so far on the climb was beyond description. I had seen and heard the most amazing things—those with MS and Parkinson's continued to climb each day without complaint and I had the privilege to hear their individual life stories along the way.

Watching Nathan or any of the other climbers left me utterly speechless. They took each day one step at a time in the most literal sense. For the first time in my life, I felt completely in the moment along with what I can only describe as serenity and contentment. It ended up being the biggest thing I took from the journey—living in the moment, one step at a time. I've since had "one at a time" tattooed across my ten toes—one letter for each toe—as a reminder of the lesson I learned.

The sunrise in the morning at that altitude was stunning. What a privilege to actually see a sunrise before those on the ground did. Even more amazing was the shadow of Kilimanjaro on the morning horizon as the sun rose behind it. I had never seen anything like that before. We left shortly after sunrise to push to High Camp where we would regroup and rest before making the final assent to the summit that evening. This leg of the climb was brutal—five hours on what seemed like trails that were almost vertical terrain of scree. After climbing this loose rock, similar to walking in sand, I was extremely tired and fearful that I might not have it in me to summit.

We rested for about seven hours—and I use that term lightly, as it was next to impossible to rest at 16,000 feet. It was even harder to rest when it was obvious that some of us weren't taking the opportunity to sleep. Normally, I would have found it funny that others wanted to pull an "all-nighter," but at this altitude with the hardest portion of the climb in front of us, their sounds were just another distraction that kept me from getting the rest I needed. I did my best to put aside my irritation and try to sleep, knowing my attitude would also play into what was to come. Apparently, others had heard the night's sounds as well, and we had a good laugh about it, which in and of itself was really difficult at 16,000 feet. Everything was challenging at that height; even zipping up a sleeping bag took all of our energy and strength.

As I contemplated what lie ahead, I recall thinking to myself that there really wasn't any way I could have properly trained for this climb. It was simply the hardest thing I had ever attempted. I credit the group and my desire to get everything I possibly could out of the experience for getting me to the top. I simply wasn't going to give up. They would have had to carry me off the mountain, because I knew I intended to continue climbing for as long as it took. Little did I know how much that idea would be tested as we pushed for the summit.

We had started that day at sunrise and hiked five hours to High Camp. We rested a bit, and then it was time to make our summit attempt. We left camp around 11:30 p.m. in the hopes of summiting around sunrise the following morning. The trail was comprised almost entirely of extremely steep switchbacks that we had to navigate in complete darkness. Our headlamps illuminated little more than the heels of the person in front of us as we leaned forward and trudged up the mountain. I am not sure when things started to get bad, but in my journal I wrote it was about three to four hours into the ascent. It was cold, extremely steep, pitch black, and seemed to never end.

Our group of five to six split from our main group because we were moving a bit faster. At that point the group started to fall apart, myself included. We had to give Nathan's pack to our guide. We were all zombies. Members of our group started to talk about quitting. I was in a ton of pain and started to mentally disconnect in order to carry on. I had to keep reminding myself to stay focused and stay in the moment. As I repeated it to myself, I took the opportunity to say it out loud to the group in order to encourage everyone.

Once we were close to Stella Point, about an hour-and-a-half from the summit, I dug into the group hard. I said a lot of things I couldn't remember by the time I got to my journal, but I know it included anything I could think of to keep everyone motivated and moving forward. Truthfully, it was really just me convincing myself to carry on, but I said it out loud hoping it would also help someone other than me. When we could see Stella Point, I grabbed Nathan and ran as hard as I could up the trail to the checkpoint. I helped Nathan sit down, threw off my pack, and ran back down to help carry anyone else who needed assistance. Once our small group reached Stella Point we rested for five to ten minutes and then pressed on. We knew if we rested any longer, we would not only miss the sunrise, but we might not make the summit.

For me, the time on the summit was both amazing and insanely difficult. The altitude had not been much of a factor, but it hit me hard once we reached the summit. I was disoriented, had a crazy headache, and was completely exhausted. In addition, the joy of reaching the summit was quickly overshadowed by the fact that the summit is only half the journey—a very long climb back down awaited me.

The views atop Kilimanjaro were stunning. There were more people than I expected on the summit and there was a wait to get our pictures taken with the famous sign. We waited, took our pictures, shared some tears, and geared up for our climb back down.

The trip back to High Camp almost broke me. I was more exhausted than I had ever been in my life and was simply drained in every way. By the time I got back down to camp, Nathan was having difficulty with his medication. He had to switch up the timing, and because of that, coupled with the fact that his metabolism was working in overtime, he became very symptomatic. After resting for a couple of hours, the group left to head down to the camp where we would sleep that evening. I and a guide each took one of Nathan's arms and literally ran down to 12,500 feet. Nathan couldn't keep his momentum from shifting forward, which led us into a jog down the trail. We were lucky no one broke an ankle or worse, but we made it down to the next camp and rested.

Funny thing about the camp at 12,500 feet...you can

buy a beer. I had actually been able to put my demons and urges aside during the climb, but as soon as I knew there was beer, I was all over it. I did my best to not overindulge, but that was hard. I had this sense of entitlement—this belief that I deserved however many I wanted. I had saved a couple of Percocet and took them that evening too. I melted into my sleeping bag, self-satisfied with my climbing achievement and believing I deserved every drop of those beers and each of those pills.

We awoke early the next morning and hiked down the rest of the mountain. We were greeted by the villagers at the trailhead who welcomed us with songs and dancing. It was one of the coolest things I have ever experienced. We finished that day with a cookout in the village to celebrate our accomplishment. It was a fitting end to an amazing experience. I was able to come out of my place of solitude long enough to bond with many people in the group.

I learned so much from my fellow climbing partners. After our summit, I had felt justified in indulging in alcohol and pills, but once I got home, I began to realize the distortion of that thought process. The time on the mountain served as the beginning of my realization that I didn't need drugs or alcohol to be "loose." I didn't need those things in order to come out of my shell and connect with another human being.

Of everything and everyone who impacted me on the trip, most of all, I want to thank my climbing partner, Nathan, for showing me what true strength is. Nathan served as my biggest inspiration. He was able to climb one of the tallest mountains in the world with a movement disorder. Not only that, but he did it without complaining even once. That accomplishment, when compared to my belief that my disease of addiction defined who I was, helped me realize how wrong I had been. I don't have to let my struggle define and control my life just as Nathan didn't let Parkinson's define or control his.

I was able to take home with me the example he showed on the trip, along with my other experiences from the climb. This truly did turn out to be *the thing bigger than me that finally began to put my life into perspective— in more ways than I ever imagined.* Although I didn't get sober right away, I am happy to say that as of this writing, I am seven months sober, and enjoying with my wife our one-year-old adopted daughter Harper. I am happier than I have ever been. Thank you, Nathan, and thank you fellow Leap of Faith friends.

Daniel Wilkins is an advertising executive living in Atlanta with his wife, daughter and two dogs. He co-founded the Wilkins Parkinson's Foundation in 2010 with his father who was diagnosed with Parkinson's disease in 2006. He is an active runner, mountain climber and Brazilian Jujitsu competitor.

Doing Things and Meeting People I Never Dreamed Of

Paula Sanchez

IT IS TRULY INCREDIBLE HOW THE THREADS OF life can weave amazing and unexpected paths. The first person I knew with MS was the mother of a friend I have known since elementary school, Mrs. Tinebra. I remember Mrs. Tinebra walking with a little difficulty but it wasn't anything alarming, at least not to a grade schooler. Then, Mrs. Tinebra needed crutches to walk. Ultimately, she was confined to a wheelchair. I witnessed this progression throughout grade school and high school.

I think of how my friend, Tricia, along with her four other siblings and their father, all pitched in around the house to help Mrs. Tinebra with whatever was needed. No complaints. Stoic, steadfast, and unwavering in support of their loved one. I have carried these memories with me throughout the years and think of Mrs. Tinebra and her family often.

Fast forward to the new millennium. My involvement with MS started in 2001. A co-worker, Colleen, asked me to sponsor her in a three-day, fifty-mile walk, the MS Challenge Walk, that she was embarking on for the Northern California National MS Society. I thought, "Wow! Fifty miles. That is quite a feat!"

After the walk, Colleen regaled us with stories of how she passed the time walking so many miles, the people she met and their MS stories, the crazy costumes and accessories the walkers and volunteers wore, and the various activities throughout the weekend. This event was life changing and empowering for her. Colleen's excitement about her experiences and inspiration from the walk were contagious. By the end of the walk weekend, Colleen had already decided she would be walking again the following year.

I asked what she would do different for the next year, if anything, to enhance her experience. I was thinking along the lines of different shoes, more sunscreen, maybe a costume, different fundraising ideas, more/less training, etc. She looked into the air, with her index finger on her cheek, and with a mischievous grin turned to me and said, "The only thing that will make it better is if you walk with me!" *Ha! Right! Me, walk 50 miles? I don't think so. It's much easier to donate and cheer from the sidelines.*

Colleen's enthusiasm for the walk made quite an impression on me, however. Her suggestion to walk the next year planted a seed, and over the next few months I couldn't get it out of my mind. I finally made the decision to participate in the 2002 MS Challenge Walk, to get on with the business of training and fundraising and really get involved. I've now walked with Colleen for ten years and dream of a day when there is a cure for her and everyone afflicted with MS. No more suffering—no more pain. It is our fervent wish. My teammates and I are friends of the heart, united by one goal—a world free of MS.

Our involvement with the National MS Society has taken me back to my childhood and my memories of the Tinebra family many times. As I've learned about MS—its symptoms, progression, and treatments—I've wondered whether Mrs. Tinebra encountered these or other pathologies, what treatments she has undergone, and the success of those treatments. The Tinebras are always in my heart and often in my thoughts. I continue to carry them with me on every MS-related walk and event.

The year 2011 was filled with excitement, new opportunities, and significant life-changing events. I've had a lifelong dream of visiting Africa, being intrigued by the animals, landscape, history, and people. When I learned about the Leap of Faith Kilimanjaro trip, it felt like kismet. I never could have imagined that I would have the opportunity to combine MS advocacy with my dream of visiting Africa. I had seen the May 2009 picture of Lori Schneider on World MS Day, summiting Everest and holding the World MS flag. I wanted to know more about her and began to follow her on Facebook. When Lori announced the trip on Facebook, I contacted her with lots of questions to understand what would be required for this trip. Lori graciously fielded every one of my laundry list of questions and was immensely encouraging. Since I had never hiked before, I really had no idea what was involved. Was it a technical climb or not? Could my dream really become reality? I could hardly believe it! Once it became clear that I actually *could* hike Kili, I embarked on an amazing, uplifting, and life-defining journey.

I had so many hopes and dreams for this adventure, but I had no idea how much it would touch my heart and spirit! I was excited to have a forum to get the word out about MS. I wanted MS to be as recognizable as cancer so there would be more donations, funding, and ultimately, a cure. MS isn't as common or as identifiable as cancer. In the past, I had received quizzical looks from people when I mentioned the MS Walk. "Is that what so-and-so actor/actress has?" was a common reaction. One person even thought MS was the same as muscular dystrophy, for which the Jerry Lewis telethon is known. With this climb, I had the opportunity to educate people further and encourage them to support advancements toward a cure.

The goodwill and camaraderie were present from the very beginning of the trip. Most of us were strangers before this adventure began, and when we met, there was an instant bond. The shared stories, triumphs, losses, hopes, dreams, information exchange, and learnings tied our team together in heart and soul. Within the first couple days of the trip, there was already talk of a reunion!

The selflessness and "all for one" attitude exhibited by our team were heartening to witness. The compassion was endless. If one of us needed assistance, many teammates dropped their packs and ran over to see what they could do to help. We were all getting up that mountain and we were doing it together.

One instance that epitomized what this trip was all about was when one of our PD climbers rolled into our break area in excruciating pain. She was in tears and we were fearful she might not be able to continue. We all crowded around to see how we could help and offered our love and encouragement. Her pain was in her upper back and Stephanie, one of the MS climbers who was also a physical therapy student at the time, pondered aloud whether a massage might alleviate some of her discomfort. Within a few minutes after Stephanie began to gently massage our team member's back, I could see some relief wash over her face. It seemed to be working. We all crossed our fingers. When our rest break was over and we were ready to move on, Stephanie decided to stay back and continue caring for our "team member in need." The rest of us pressed on, grateful for Stephanie's caring and expertise. This was an incredibly touching and heartwarming moment.

I was along on this trip as a companion climber to Stephanie. Stephanie was a very experienced climber, while I was a complete novice—a big concern for me because I wanted and needed to be there for Steph and offer my assistance to her. Being her support person had motivated me immensely in my training. I did not want to let Steph down. I wanted to be there for her every step of the way.

At times, I felt Stephanie gave me so much more than I gave her. I was there to help her up the mountain and yet, she was the one showing me how to use gear, graciously imparting hiking wisdom, and offering guidance. At the Machame gate, we waited around to check in and pay our fees before starting our climb. Stephanie, noticing that my gaiters were on backwards, politely pointed this out and graciously helped me get them on correctly. Boy was I embarrassed!

I've always felt guilty about my inexperience and not being the type of resource I had hoped to be for Steph. A friend, however, had an eye-opening observation when I relayed my story—the reversal of roles and the opportunity for Steph to help me may have been more valuable to her than I realized. I hope I gave Stephanie the support she needed and desired. Without a doubt, she gave me so much more than I ever imagined, and I am forever grateful to her for her guidance and unending support.

I thank Sean, one of the MS climbers, for encouraging us to forge on when we didn't think we could go another step on summit night. I remember one instance on that long, cold, dark night, during one of our rest breaks, when all I wanted to do was slip behind a rock to lie down and curl up. Because it was bitter cold, that was all I could think about. I heard Sean's shouts of encouragement and they propelled me onward. It was incredibly empowering to realize I could do more than I ever thought possible. It was also sobering and frightening to see how our bodies reacted to the altitude and lack of oxygen. My head was pounding and my heart felt as if it were beating out of my chest. I'm not sure which was winning the contest but they were both in contention.

Many of my hopes and dreams were realized on this trip. There were also some unexpected outcomes. All great. The depth of camaraderie, as well as the hope and sense of accomplishment were more than I could have imagined. I knew this would be an incredible trip, but it turned out to be so much more than my expectations. I have always had a very positive outlook on life. Yet, this climb enhanced my positivity exponentially. We call it the "Kili high." It's hard to describe but it was an incredibly happy and fulfilling time for me.

It's pretty amazing to think I've gone from knowing one or two people with MS to interacting with hundreds and to being part of an inspiring adventure halfway around the world. Our MS and PD climbers changed what it means to live with an illness and have given hope to people around the world. The amazing people I met on the Kili trip and the exchange of stories, treatments, and hopes between us were incredibly uplifting.

What I learned about myself will stay with me forever as well. After training for many months and sharing my progress with family and friends, I was very motivated to reach the summit. In the early days of the climb, however, reaching the summit stopped being a personal priority. We focused our efforts to support the climbers with MS and Parkinson's. Every step they took was a successful, history-making moment. This was our chance to show the world that living with a disease does not mean an end to adventure or physical activity—it means that there is always hope. Suz, one of our companion climbers, said it perfectly, "Every day is summit day." It did not matter how far anyone made it—what mattered is that we all tried and reached our highest potential. It was an incredibly successful trip, regardless of who did or didn't summit. Ultimately, we all reached our personal summits.

Like most people, I was focused on a goal and the Kili trip showed me what's truly most important. It's the journey and the people you meet along the way that count most. Yes, it was quite an accomplishment to reach the top, but I treasure the friendships with my teammates even more. The bond we formed continues today.

The people I've met that live with MS and PD have shown me what it really means to live fully. Yes, their diagnoses were frightening and debilitating initially but they've emerged triumphant, successful, and happy. If ever faced with adversity, I hope to take on my challenge in the same manner as my teammates.

I have been deeply touched by the inspiring people I met and lived with for two weeks. This experience continues to spur on my involvement even further. After the climb, I do not know how or why, but I am more committed to an MS cure than ever before. A cure has always been urgent. The elusiveness of a cure is so frustrating, but we will not give up. The longer I participate in MS events, the more entrenched and invested I become in the community and a cure. I cannot turn away. The sense of community, determination, transformation, and triumph I witnessed on this trip are indelibly etched in my heart, as are the amazing companions who took this leap of faith alongside me. I am forever changed by my connection to MS and Parkinson's.

Paula Sanchez *loves travel, adventure, nature and animals. Paula is a native Californian and resides in Tracy, California with her husband, Michael, and their two beloved* *pooches, Chloe and Sami. Paula has been bitten by the hiking-trekking bug. Upcoming adventures include ice climbing, hiking Volcanoes in Iceland, along with dreams of trekking Annapurna, running in The Great Wall of China Half Marathon and many more adventures!*

A Long Journey

"The journey of a thousand miles begins with a single step."
- Lao Tzu

Pushing the Limits

Nathan S. Henwood

FIVE O'CLOCK IN THE MORNING. IT'S COLD, DARK, and I am tired. We've been hiking behind our guide for the past seven-plus hours. It doesn't sound like much, but considering we've only had two hours to rest and this is Day Six of the climb, it is a lot. My headlamp is pointed down at the back of our guide's old, well-used hiking boots. His gait is shorter than mine so I have to wait for him to take two steps before I can take one. The white light from the LED bulb is bright—a cold light that matches the cold temperature of the thin air. The shadows to the left and right of me are alive with figments of my imagination. As soon as I look closer, the shapes vanish.

Step after step, I swing my ski poles as I walk. It seems as if we will never reach the top of this endless slope. I don't care that my back hurts or that I can't catch my breath. I need to go on step after step. I am like a machine—my leg moving my heavy boot to a solid spot, arm swinging the pole like a weapon stabbing into the rock. I turned off the part of me that said "you can't do this anymore" awhile back. Behind me, no one is talking. The air is too thin, and we are just too tired to waste the energy on even a few words. I can hear my own breathing and wonder if everyone else can hear it too. My water bottle is hanging from my shoulder strap, swinging with every step I take, slowly freezing solid in the cold of the night.

Behind me is Daniel, my climbing partner. As always, like a cat, he is ready to spring forward and steady me if I slip or lose my balance. Though I just met Daniel a week ago, we have become fast friends. I try to be careful as I climb, for his sake and mine. On and on we travel up the mountain. With each glance up, the top of the slope seems even further away. Finally, we stop at a level spot in the dark, by a sign that reads, "You are at Stella Point ALT 5730 Meters." We have just reached the 18,799-foot level on Mount Kilimanjaro in Tanzania, Africa.

We are ecstatic, thinking we are nearly there. Daniel and I look at the sign, then hug and cry a few tears until we are told it will be another hour to gain the last 550 feet to the top. From here, we will have to travel around the massive crater along the rim to get us to the summit. Our guides, in addition to lugging heavy packs with extra supplies, also brought up warm thermos bottles filled with hot coffee. Thankfully, we take our last break before we begin the push to the top. We drink the hot coffee and enjoy the warmth in the cold as we huddle near a rocky wall off the trail.

Again we set out for the top of Africa and the tallest freestanding mountain in the world. Though the trail is fairly level, it doesn't matter. The cold, thin air and lack of sleep make each step feel as if we are trying to complete a marathon.

My camera swings like an anchor around my neck, but I am used to it. Photography has always been my passion. My fingers are so cold that it is extremely difficult to turn the camera on. The sun is just starting to rise in the eastern sky—shades of pink, yellow, and red cresting over the crater rim. I take a few shots but am quickly herded along by my cold fellow climbers. We are nearly there.

As we approach, all I can think about is how tired I am and how I won't possibly have enough energy for the return trip. But I push those thoughts to the side. *First get to the top, then worry about turning around,* I chide myself. *I need to do this. I am not, and will not, be limited by Parkinson's disease.*

I know I am not only doing this for me—I am also here for anyone else who has Parkinson's. Our group has ten people with multiple sclerosis and four with Parkinson's. It's clear we *can* do more than most people believe possible. Even more than most doctors think. A person may be locked inside a body with a degenerative disease, but we have the power to not let it define us. I was 46 years old when I was diagnosed. At 54, I am now more and more convinced that Parkinson's is not going to stop me. I will work as hard as necessary to keep going.

Soon we are so close to the top—I can smell it. Gina, one of the MS climbers, is close behind me, along with Daniel. They both look exhausted; I'm wondering if I look as drained as they do. A breath with a step—then two, three, or four more with each additional step. This goes on and on. In the distance, I see that people are clustered around the summit. I look down at my feet and don't know where the power will come to keep moving.

Daniel, Gina, and I arrive at the summit of Mount Kilimanjaro—19,340 feet of utter pain and joy. I stand there in awe of what we have just done and the reality of the scene before me. Looking out for hundreds of miles in any direction, we see an ocean of clouds and haze. Kilimanjaro looms over three-and-a-half miles high, dominating its surroundings. Glaciers surround the flanks of the mountain—hundreds of feet thick, bright white on top and cobalt blue in the core. Sadly, I take in that, like polar bears, these glaciers are in jeopardy of disappearing completely from the world. Kilimanjaro's glaciers are predicted to be gone in just two decades.

Forty or fifty people are crowded around the summit sign as we approach. Daniel and I shake hands and hug, the sunlight thankfully covering my misty eyes. Our group photographer, Jeff, is at the top, heroically taking pictures of everyone hour after hour. It is a good thing that he is here because I am too tired and emotional to take any pictures myself. Besides, I have something else I must do.

Daniel and I unfold a banner for the Wilkins PD Foundation, named after Daniel's dad who also has Parkinson's. I start to dig around in my backpack for the three flags I've brought along with me from Washington State. I have a flag for the Moose Lodge where I and many of my supportive friends are members, in Montesano, Washington. They have all been rooting for me as I've climbed the mountain, and I can feel their support even half a world away.

I have two other flags with me that are for Jim, a veteran soldier and one of my best friends. I attach the flags to my ski poles and wave them high in the thin air over Kilimanjaro. A flood of feeling overwhelms me for all the soldiers at Fort Lewis in Washington State. I couldn't be part of the great sacrifices they have made for our country, but I want to honor them with this gesture.

We get as many of our group as possible in front of the two poles holding the weathered summit sign for our photo. We've all trained for months, paid thousands of dollars, and shed much sweat and tears to get here. Standing at the summit, a profound idea takes root, immediately becoming real to me—*any of us, with the power of belief in ourselves and hard work, can change our own lives.* The other idea—that someone's life is over because they have a "scary" disease—is finished. It is our own mind that defines the limits in our life. Sure, there are limits that are physical and mental. But we can change the boundaries of those limits. Physical handicaps, like missing limbs, are only limited by the person's ability to adapt to these challenges.

After a satisfying break at the summit, we get our things together and decide to head back to Stella Point and then down to High Camp, where we'd started at 10:45 p.m. the previous night. It is now 8:45 a.m. With the morning light, the trip back feels completely new. On the ascent, the world had been a dark, single line of headlamps providing the only illumination. Now, the bright light and intense radiation of the sun are starting to beat down on us. We had passed other groups from all over the world on the way to the top, and I wonder if they came to this mountain for themselves or for some larger purpose.

On the way down, I start to stagger from side to side. My medication, and maybe the altitude, is having an effect on me. I am walking more like a drunk than a mountain climber. The air is thin and hard to breath, but at least we have gravity to help us down the trail. I see one of my fellow climbers, a 65-year-old woman with Parkinson's, along with her guide, coming toward us. She and I trained together, and she is an amazing and inspiring woman. I give her a big hug and tell her how proud I am of her—and that she is almost there.

We are getting close to Stella Point, so we move around the rim of the crater to a high point of rock. We stop and have some much-needed water and a little to eat. At this altitude, we get very dried out. The ground around us is barren of life or water. There is a lot of radiation from the intense sunlight, plus everything gets kind of freeze dried at night. The dust isn't too bad because it's early in the morning and the wind hasn't yet picked up. I think of how miserable it would be up here in the wind with the dust and sand flying through the air.

After a short break, I get up and walk to the trail near the sign for Stella Point. One of our guides, also named Daniel, asks if I am ready to go. I reply "sure," not knowing what to expect. "Give me your left ski pole; you hold the right," he instructs. We look down a slope from Stella Point that we hadn't been able to see in the dark on the way up. Then I remember the briefing we'd received. Our head guide, Eric, had talked about the gravel shoots we would slide down on the way back. I'm not quite sure what to expect, but I believe I'm ready.

I seem to have more energy now after the short rest.

We are using the Mweka route to descend the mountain, and I feel ready for this part of the adventure. I am glad we didn't climb it on the way up, because it is filled with miles of volcanic gravel—one to four inches in size. Daniel and I, arm-in-arm, go over the edge of the crater's rim and head down the steep slope, starting at 18,799 feet. My climbing partner and another guide come down after us. With our poles flying, and still arm-in-arm, we use our feet like skis, sliding down the mountain. We kick up clouds of dust, and the gravel sounds like thousands of hollow marbles moving downward with us. *At least we'll get down the mountain quickly,* I think, *and hopefully in one piece.* We don't stop at all as we continue down the gravel slopes. When I look back, all I can see is a giant dust cloud following us from the top of the mountain.

I spot our camp below; it looks completely different from this vantage point. I remember the climb briefing and the schedule of our trip. I realize that I will be back at High Camp around 10:00 a.m., then we will break camp sometime after 2:00 or 3:00 p.m. to descend to Mweka camp, situated at 12,500 feet. Looking at High Camp, I think—for the briefest moment—that we're already about to make it to the lower Mweka campsite. I think I see the trees and brush surrounding the camp. Just as quickly, I realize that this is my mind hoping we've come further than we actually have, so that I can sleep for hours to recharge my body. *It is wishful thinking;* I have to admit to myself.

Daniel and I are almost through the gravel slide. Like a sailor getting off a ship, my legs continue to hold me up but they are now incapable of slowing me down. Daniel doesn't understand that I have passed the point where my legs work in any way beyond holding me upright. This horrifies me, thinking that aides might have to come up and cart me down the last mile to High Camp. Daniel must have begun to sense what is happening to me, because he spots another of our guides, Ronald, and asks that he give us a hand.

Daniel and Ronald hold me by each arm and guide me down the last mile of the mountain to High Camp. I still don't know where Daniel, my climbing companion, is. I am trying to remain standing for these guys, but I don't think they understand fully what is going on—that I have no control over slowing myself down. It's as if I have no muscles at all for any kind of movement. Still arm-in-arm, we stumble into camp. They put me in a chair and give me some orange juice. I can't even get up from the chair. Another team member helps me into my tent to lie down and rest. I am thinking, *This is it; I have used up every bit of energy from every single cell in my body.*

As exhausted as I feel, though, I am still concerned about Daniel, my partner—he hasn't made it in yet. I feel guilty for not staying closer together on the descent. Although it seems like it took forever, Daniel makes it into camp soon after me. Having made it to the top of the mountain and now lying on my sleeping bag, I consider how ready I am to stop—to not take another step in any direction. I know my medication has been at least two times the dosage I usually need. Coupled with the altitude and the stress of the climb, I understand this isn't good.

A few hours later, with everyone back at camp, I hear that 21 of the 28 climbers in our group made it to the top of the mountain. I realize that the important thing is we have all tried and every one of us made it further than most healthy people could have done. We have achieved what most consider impossible.

As we get ready to leave camp, April, one of our MS climbers, is having a bad go of it. She made it to High Camp, but I'm not sure that she made it any further up the mountain. The guides and porters put her on a stretcher to transport her down the mountain. She's 27 years old and has a severe case of progressive MS. I know she did more than anyone thought she could. She is truly an amazing woman; I am proud to have been one of her climbing companions. April is securely strapped into a basket with lots of blankets covering her and six to eight porters and guides all around. There is a single tire at the bottom of the basket. I wonder whether the rough trail ahead is a good thing for April but trust that the care she is receiving will be what she needs.

Eric, our head guide, asks me if I think I can make it the rest of the way down. What else could I say but "yes"? I don't want to be a burden on anyone. *After all*, I consider, *we all have the same thing on our plates.* I do feel a little better at the moment but that will soon change.

From what I'd heard previously, the trail down the mountain is one way—a creek bed that no longer has any water in it, and it goes straight down the mountain—over boulders, cracks in the earth, and even dry waterfalls. About two-thirds of the way down to the next camp, I need one of the guides on one side of me, with my partner, Daniel, on the other. This is quite a scene as these guys help me through a sloped trail filled with boulders and rocks that is only wide enough for one or two of us to pass at one time—not the three of us moving along side-by-side.

We could have been doing this at a company picnic, I think, because we look like a three-legged foot race in motion. We have to take turns walking over the rocks. My legs continue to keep me erect but once again, the power to slow down is gone. We "race" our way down towards Mweka camp, with the air becoming distinctly thicker as we progress. The small shrubs have even returned to the landscape. We see clouds below us and the foliage is becoming denser and taller, until it forms large, sparse bushes and small trees.

The porters who have taken care of us throughout the trip pass us to reach Mweka camp first. By the time we bound in, our tents are almost completely set up. We find a tent, and I sit in a chair that has been brought to me. This is our camp for the night—a good place for me to recuperate.

We gather in a group at one of our group member's tents. When we arrived at camp, we found out we could buy beer at the trading post. We all enjoy a few beers, each other's company, and the lower altitude. After resting for a few hours I begin to feel better, but my muscles are still tired to the bone. I don't think I've ever been this tired. I think to myself that there is only one more day and we will be off the mountain. The porters and guides serve authentic foods of the area, but I am too tired to move from my sleeping bag. I'm sure there are a number of us who can't make it to the meal.

The last morning on the mountain we eat and pack up our stuff. The trail becomes more like a "regular trail" as we wind our way down the rest of the mountain. The plants and terrain change as we enter the wet rainforest.

We all start to call this part of the trail the Highway to Hell because of the downward slope and some of the steps that drop us one-and-a-half feet at a time. The light rain makes the jungle beautiful and the trail slippery. We pass a lot of porters who are heading up the mountain. They carry supplies for the trading post and for others on the mountain. This is one of the only times I see any native women on the trail. They seem to pack on their heads as heavy a load as the men.

We finally get to a road that curves its way down the mountain towards the exit gate. This road has become rutted from the trucks that came up for April. We slip and slide down the muddy road and finally make it to a point just before the exit gate.

As we approach the exit gate on Kilimanjaro, we hear about 200 locals singing and cheering for our group. It is the best feeling I could have ever imagined—pure joy, satisfaction, and elation. Here we are—fourteen climbers who have MS or PD, along with our fourteen companions, two doctors, and one writer/photographer in The Leap of Faith Expedition. We have just spent eight days on the mountain, traveled 40 miles, climbed to 19,340 feet—surpassing our wildest dreams of what we thought we could accomplish.

This is the finish line for the trip of a lifetime. We have climbed the tallest mountain on the continent of Africa. And now we are all singing and dancing in the streets. The group of locals meets us in song and dance. One of the locals meets each of us with a smile and places an orange flower lei around our necks. Some of our group is dancing at the gateway from the mountain. It is a joyous celebration of the hard work we have just finished.

We are escorted to an area near the gate where we can relax and eat some food that has been made especially for us. There are lots of locals who want to sell things to us. They are everywhere around the area, selling carvings, flags, paintings, and more. As we rest and eat, a couple of locals take off our boots to wash them. They work for the hotel in Arusha where we will stay.

At first, we don't know what to think about this gesture, but Eric assures us it is okay. We enjoy the pampering and drink a few more Kilimanjaro beers as we walk around in stocking feet. As much as I hate to say it, it is nice to be off the mountain.

After we return to our hotel in Arusha, we all take long, much-needed showers. As a group, we trek into the countryside of Tanzania on safari for the next three days. To top it off, we take a hot air balloon ride over the Serengeti at sunrise...*but that's another story.*

I remember one particular day during my training for the trip. My wife and I were driving to our place on Hood Canal in Washington State. I tell her that I feel blessed for having Parkinson's disease.

Parkinson's has opened my eyes to a whole new world. As a retired person, due to my Parkinson's, I get to do the things I love. Before PD, I would never have gone to Mt. Kilimanjaro or Africa. Because of PD, I can now help others who are dealing with similar issues. I can offer them hope. PD has given my life more meaning than it ever had before. I feel truly blessed for this life.

Although this was an incredible and amazing journey, I do think my next adventure will be closer to home, somewhere here in Washington State. Look for me on the Pacific Crest Trails in the Cascades, from Washington to California.

Nathan S Henwood *was born in Portland, Oregon in 1956. He comes from a loving family and has four sisters and three brothers. His family moved around a lot when he was school aged, which became a valuable part of his education. He acquired his passion for the outdoors and photography from his father and mother. Nathan has raised two beautiful daughters and two wonderful stepkids plus some fantastic grandchildren. In 2004, his first symptoms of Parkinson's disease came on. Nathan retired in 2009, having worked for Weyerhaeuser Lumber Co. for 34 years. He is married to Robbie, who has stood with him through the surgeries and tremors. You can contact Nathan at nathan.henwwod53@gmail.com or visit his website at http://www.nathanhenwood.com.*

It's All About
the Journey

Susie Weber

IT SEEMS MY LIFE IS ALWAYS POINTING ME IN SOME new direction. I tend to follow my heart and try to embrace and recognize new opportunities when they present themselves. Life has certainly provided me with some obstacles along the way. My life changed forever when I was diagnosed with multiple sclerosis in 1987. I used to say that I've worked very hard to never let my MS define me. How ironic is that? I realize now that that's exactly what it's done. It DOES define me—not by the negative aspects of the disease, but by the positive way I tackle life.

You don't need to know I have MS to recognize that I am very compassionate and have an extraordinary amount of personal drive. It would seem that MS has actually made me a better person. My youngest son is on the autism spectrum, my daughter has been struggling with ADHD since first grade, and my oldest son became insulin dependent at age eight. Because of my experience with MS, I am better equipped than most to endure these challenges and guide my children over their latest hurdles. In turn, they have become amazing people in and of themselves.

About six years ago, I decided to try exercising again. I wanted to see if my body would cooperate. When I was first diagnosed with MS my doctor recommended that I not exercise or do any activities that elevated my body temperature. Some people with MS have a temporary worsening of MS symptoms when they become overheated, whether from sun, fever, hot showers, or exercise. Even a slight temperature increase impairs the ability of a demyelinated nerve to conduct the necessary electrical impulses. Although that phenomenon still existed, the more recent research showed that exercise might be worth pursuing because of potential benefits for the brain and body.

Although I could barely walk a mile when I started, I was determined to improve. Since 2006, I have completed seven half marathons and participate in community fun runs whenever possible. I am not a star, but find that I am a positive role model, especially when I influence others to be healthier in some small way. Running makes me healthier; the MS makes me stronger.

Until recently, only my closest friends and long-time associates were aware of my health challenges. I wanted to build my reputation and business on the quality and creativity of my work. I saw no benefit in sharing my personal struggles and was afraid that learning about my disease might make people apprehensive about working together. By deciding to participate in the Kilimanjaro climb I guess I was finally ready to tell my story. I think my clients actually respected me more when they found out about the MS. Many are still amazed that I was able to hide my situation for as long as I did.

It was time to offer inspiration and hope to others with MS so they could see that they, too, can live life to its fullest. One way I began to share my story was through a daily blog (www.morethanamountain.net). I posted my training schedule and wrote about my MS experiences and encounters. I also needed to raise funds in order to do the climb, so Lori encouraged me to sell limited edition prints of the watercolor I had created for the header of my site.

The Kili climb was a great opportunity for me to raise awareness and learn more about both neurological diseases—MS and PD. I know this experience has made me stronger in more ways than I am able to fully appreciate. These days, my husband, friends, and family just smile when I tackle new goals, which run the spectrum from artistic projects like concrete sculptures made out of recycled/found objects to mud runs for breast cancer. All of this reaffirms my belief that each of us can take away something positive as a result of having MS in our lives and accomplish more than we know.

It is bittersweet to remember some of the experiences from our Kilimanjaro adventure. Somehow I want to be back on the mountain. Maybe it's because my life is so chaotic and I seek respite. Maybe it's because I saw what was possible for me and the others on the trip. Or maybe it's because as I reflect on the experiences of the climb I glean more insight into MS and PD. Each day, without being there, I seem to continue learning more about how the Kili climb has enriched my life. Not a day goes by without me gaining more understanding from this incredible adventure.

Ready or not, here we come.

It took forever to sort through our gear and re-swizzle our belongings to be more efficient and practical. The large conference room where we gathered looked like a yard sale on a windy day—stuff was scattered everywhere. Our gear, clothes, and snacks covered the floor of the room from wall to wall. All the pre-trip obsessing and checklist reviews no longer mattered. If I didn't have what I needed at that point, I would either have to come up with a different solution or make do without.

Not only was I most definitely one of the rookies in the group, I was also seriously lacking some much-needed sleep. Without a chance to rejuvenate from the 22-hour flight, I didn't know how my body would react to the altitude or whether my muscles would cooperate. In addition, I knew sleep deprivation makes focusing and retaining information difficult for even healthy people. Every day I am plagued by severe MS fatigue. The fatigue I endure is because of the demyelination process that's going on in my central nervous system. They call this "lassitude," and it's an overwhelming kind of tiredness not directly related to an increase in activity or something else like depression.

I kept wondering when we would have a chance to catch a quick nap but it seemed there was no extra time for that in our aggressive schedule. I was struggling to stay awake. That night I finally slept a little, although I occasionally woke in anticipation of the morning departure or with a jolt of MS-related leg spasms. Even though I had trained religiously and felt physically sound, I knew that my lassitude issue put me at a disadvantage before we even began the climb.

Our team was comprised of many people with previous climbing experience and natural athletic ability, along with a couple of super outdoorsy folks and a few who possessed the ability to spout off Tanzanian trivia and mountaineering terms as if they were second languages. I took copious notes and even drew diagrams of survival tips like how to treat the cap and rim of our water bottles. Purifying the water we drank was essential, and forgetting to treat the cap could cause problems later. All I can say is thank God for UV sani-pens. It made the whole process much easier. While some people had to use iodine drops and let their water sit before they could drink it, the UV pen didn't use chemicals and only took about a minute to purify the water. My water tasted pretty good and helped me stay adequately hydrated.

By the time we arrived at the gate of the mountain our group was eager and ready. Most seemed relaxed and comfortable with their equipment. I was still a bit out of my element, being away from how I typically passed my days—running my business. No cell phone, no computer, no immediate deadlines—it took awhile to settle into the reality that I was really here. This gal with MS from Wisconsin who could only climb the stairs once a day in the 90's was now taking a leap of faith with a group of strangers to show the world what is possible.

The number one question people ask about the climb (other than, "Did you make it to the top?") is: "Where or how did you go to the bathroom on the mountain?" The roadside souvenir shops and money exchange places basically had a hole in the ground, sometimes with a pull chain flusher and a hint of porcelain if you were lucky. A group of us actually piled into the first "toilet" for a photo just to document the experience.

But on the mountain, at our first break, I had my inaugural experience. This had been a topic of much discussion before the trip within the women of our group. It was recommended that the women bring a urinary funnel for ease and convenience (a.k.a., the "Go Girl" or "PLAM"—pee like a man). On my first attempt, it became apparent that I would need more practice with this device. Who knew? I didn't navigate the direction of the wind properly and my right leg was instantly warm and wet. Fortunately, the technical fabric of my clothes dried quickly, and I never used the funnel again. I may be a bit of a princess, but by the end of the climb I could have cared less where I went, as long as it wasn't one of the public huts on the mountain. (The mere thought of those huts makes me shiver in disgust).

The other standard toileting procedure was if you "went" on the mountain, you needed to put any soiled toilet paper or tissue into a plastic bag, carry it with you all day long, and dispose of it back at base camp. Yep. That was the mantra—*leave no trace*. In the end, we understood that it was a good thing and we all did our part. Our group was incensed whenever we saw litter, especially the blue and gold candy wrappers that were clearly discarded in irreverence to the mountain. Coincidentally, those same candies were given as complimentary treats on the plane ride from the Serengeti safari to our hotel in Arusha.

Another mountain luxury at camp and lunch was the toilet tent. (Yes, the porters took good care of us). It was complete with a small plastic potty reminiscent of the toilet training years with my children. Our guide, Eric, actually provided step-by-step instruction for using the facility. Being tall, the logistics of getting in and out of the zippered tent each time was quite a feat, especially with my large-brimmed hat and headlamp on.

The second most common question I am asked about the climb is: "Where did you shower?" The answer is we didn't. That's right. Seven days without a shower. Each night the porters brought us a plastic washbowl of water. We spit our toothpaste into tissue (because it leaves a footprint), used the water, and personal wipes to clean up as best we could. I only took off my hat in the tent. My hair was pasted to my head—less than lovely, but I was just too exhausted to care. Funny how one's priorities can change.

We did not reach our first camp during daylight hours. That meant we needed to hike with our headlamps on. Even that first night, I felt the effects of altitude and could hear myself breathing like Darth Vader. I wondered how on earth I would make it to the top if I was already having trouble. I must confess, though, that using the headlamp was cool. I even bought one for each of my children at Christmas the following year. Later, one of the other team members, Jeanne, told me that she recommended headlamps as a motivator to get her young students to read.

My trip partner, Mickey, took the lead when we arrived at camp and showed me how to properly set up our stuff.

I also watched her pack and repack her things with the grace of a seasoned traveler. This was awesome since I was clueless about the ins and outs of tent camping and was grateful for her direction. For instance, we lined the perimeter with our gear to help insulate the tent and layered the bottom of the tent with a foam pad, a self-inflating pad, and my zero degree sleeping bag.

Mickey was the perfect partner. She looked out for me and made sure from day one that we were organized and that I was drinking and refueling regularly. We had many memorable moments together, but I think we enjoyed best of all waking up to the coffee and cookies that the porters delivered to our tent door each morning. One of Mickey's greatest gifts is her calm and gentle demeanor. I couldn't have had a better partner.

The second day of the climb was enjoyable, and I found myself overcome with emotion as we walked into camp. One of my teammates, Nathan, gave me a hug as tears made streak marks down my dusty cheeks. I couldn't speak. He gave me a smile, communicating that he understood. It was both an emotional and memorable moment. I kept thinking about the many people I knew with MS who were counting on me to do this climb for them and how lucky I was to be well enough to be there. I will never take this experience for granted.

Climbing the Barranco Wall was one of the many highlights of the climb for me. I felt like Spider Woman scaling that rock face. It was as if I finally knew what those long legs of mine were meant to do. I was not afraid or unsteady and felt in my element. I knew my training had been worth every bead of sweat and tender muscle.

As I climbed I thought back to two years earlier. Ironically, at our annual birthday lunch, three of my dearest friends were talking about plans for the future. That's when I casually mentioned that I hoped to climb Kilimanjaro. They were amused by this as they were still getting used to my new passion for running. We laughed about the absurdity of the whole adventure. Everything was discussed, from my fear of heights to my history of MS vision loss and less-than-athletic physique (I am clearly an artist—not an athlete). It was all in jest; we laughed until tears rolled down our cheeks. We decided summiting Kilimanjaro was a long shot, but they spurred me on. After scrambling up the wall I felt truly empowered. I *had* overcome my fear of heights after all.

On the day we headed to High Camp a dull headache and chills from the previous night left me frustrated and weak. I'd had trouble since the first night regulating my body temperature at night even though I was covered with hand and toe warmers, fully clothed, and had stuffed my puffy down coat and extra clothes inside my mummy bag for insulation. I shook so much I couldn't fall asleep for more than a few minutes. Finally, I slept with a hot water bottle. This made a tremendous difference.

There was so much dust on the mountain that I had trouble knowing if the headache was from my allergies or mountain sickness. My eyes were very red and hurt to move them. They were extremely light sensitive, and I swear the amount of glare during the day was almost crippling. I suspected I was getting iritis, which I'd had before. I also have ankylosing spondylitis, and iritis is an ailment associated with that disease. Our team's medical experts confirmed my suspicions but didn't have the right kind of eye drops along to treat my situation. Fortunately, one of our team members, Connie, had steroid drops with her and shared them with me. I don't think I would have been able to continue on without some relief. Several teammates helped administer the drops over the next few days and things improved.

The dining tent reminded many of us of the scenes in the dining hall from *Harry Potter*. Certainly not as big but it glowed from within and was like a hive buzzing with conversations. That night I was like a human bobble head at dinner. I could not stay fully awake during the nightly recap and instructions. Not sleeping well for several nights in a row, along with other incidental health symptoms that had flared up, seemed to compound my MS symptoms. I was thoroughly exhausted.

The next morning's trek became extremely difficult for me. My thoughts were cloudy, I was sluggish, and my legs felt like logs. I think it was the mountain reminding me that I live in Wisconsin where altitude is basically nonexistent. I was touched by the fact that some of our teammates in the faster group stayed back to talk with our group. Unfortunately, because I was struggling to breathe, my head was pounding, and I had taken some allergy meds, it was not possible for me to engage in any kind of meaningful conversation. All I could do was focus on each step forward.

The hours before lunch were even more difficult, and I was grateful for the ginger candy and shared stories that helped pass the time and distract me from my physical strain. My pack seemed to have doubled in weight. Two of my more experienced teammates repeatedly encouraged me to let a porter carry it. I can be stubborn but they convinced me that I would hold back the group if I couldn't go at a stronger pace. Lori had tried to persuade me as well, but it was after a conversation with her father Neal that something hit home. After lunch I gave up my pack.

One of my greatest strengths is also my greatest weakness. I am goal-oriented, driven, and stubborn—my MS has taught me to persevere. The only reason I gave up my pack was out of respect for my teammates. I did not want to hinder their performance or hold the team back in any way, yet I didn't want to contribute to the burden of the porters. This was a difficult moment for me. At first I felt like I was giving up. But I had no other choice. With the poise of ballerinas, the porters carried our boundary bags, which were about the size of dishwashers, along with everything else on their heads. They made it look graceful, and the burden of their labor was only evident by the beads of sweat that trickled down their muscular bodies. They never complained. They sang and called out "Jambo" endlessly. It's humbling to think about them even now.

Giving up my pack was when I came to terms with the fact that this trip really wasn't about summiting at all. Even though I knew the journey was the most important part of this adventure, I didn't really get it until I handed my pack over. I also recalled how I'd had difficulty walking just four months earlier due to a reaction to a prescribed MS drug. A deep sense of gratitude set in. And yes, in some twisted way this was one of the big highlights of the trip for me.

Arriving at High Camp, I knew I was in trouble and that my body wasn't cooperating like I had hoped. I knew I was having altitude issues. I really wasn't sure anymore if I would summit. It was a lot to deal with.

That night I finally took a half of a tablet of the medication used to prevent altitude sickness and told Eric I was having a few altitude issues. At dinner when the oxometer was passed around, I was barely at 80. My father had needed to monitor his oxygen levels due to lung disease so I was well aware that this number was not good.

Our group went to bed for about two hours before we began our final ascent. Our guide had me check my number again before we left, and I was clearly frustrated. There was no hiding my unhappiness at that moment, because my new oxygen levels wavered between 71 and 73. He suggested that I just see how I felt as we went. So that's what I did. Miraculously, I didn't feel any worse as we progressed but never had the opportunity to check my number again. As my friend's mom said to me once, "It's like eating an elephant...you do it one piece at a time." And that's what I did.

Because our group left at about 10:30 at night, we had our headlamps on and looked like a train of giant fireflies plodding through the boulders and scree in the darkness of the cold mountain air. The pace was slow, and I could not use my headlamp because my eyes could barely open, still hyper-sensitive to the light. I pressed my forehead on my Tanzanian guide's pack and was lulled by his singing and the rhythm of his footsteps as we slowly made our way to the false summit, Stella's Point.

By the time the sun rose we'd made it to Stella's Point and I had renewed hope that I might actually make it to the top, although the last of my water was frozen and my hands were numb and cold. I knew, however, that I could work through these things because I used to ski in colder conditions than this with my family in the Midwest.

By this time my guide, Rodman, and I had been separated from our group for about six hours. We had inched up the mountain by ourselves. My mind wandered and I tried to regain focus by thinking of the people who had inspired me to do this climb—my parents, my family, my friends, my MS peers, the people in the world who need to know that with hope everything is possible. I reverted to bible passages and hymns, and I prayed. I pondered lyrics from songs and recited rhymes from my youth. I pictured my children's faces and recalled moments in my life as if they were flashing before me like a slideshow. It's funny how all of these things gave me the strength to continue.

Meanwhile our other guide, Ben, let us know that Kristy, my friend from Wisconsin, had to be escorted down to a lower altitude. Kristy and I had known each other through our church and daughters, but became closer after her MS diagnosis. Once, when we met for coffee, we decided to bring our recent MRI films along and actually pasted our full-size brain scans on the windows and compared our lesions. It was strangely comforting, and I think we bonded for life as a result. Now, on this trip, Kristy was having a life-threatening asthma attack and I couldn't help her. I had promised her husband I would look after her, but there was nothing I could do. Thankfully, Kristy was taken down to a lower altitude where she began to recover.

Rodman and I kept going. I really didn't have a choice anymore. I refocused and reminded myself why we were doing this climb. At this point I also knew I could not make any more stops along the way or I would not make it either.

As the sun began to rise, it revealed a landscape of volcanic ash and barren of plants. The only signs of life were the comings and goings of people that seemed more like zombies than humans. I was a zombie too. My mind was fuzzy and my body moved as if on autopilot. I had on my four pairs of pants and three jackets. I looked like the Michelin tire man. In retrospect, it was a miracle I could move at all. Eventually some of my teammates recognized me when our paths crossed. They shouted words of encouragement. I don't know if I stopped at all because I was on a mission and delirium had begun to set in. Later I read in Martha's blog that my lips had turned blue and some of the others were a bit concerned.

It took forever to reach Uhuru Peak, and I could not stay to bask in the moment for even a little bit. I knew my energy reserves were almost nonexistent. I was fading fast, and I needed to start heading back down right away. Rodman took my picture, and I was grateful. As we began our descent I saw the last of my teammates going up to Uhuru. We embraced, and tears of joy filled our eyes. I felt a sense of relief to see them.

The next thing I knew, another team member was forcing me to swallow a packet of GU, the energy gel we carried, and instructing me to drink some of his water. I shudder when I think of how queasy the GU made me feel—it was difficult to keep it down. Yet, when the fuel gave me new strength, I finally noticed the awesomeness of the 50-foot glaciers that exist on the rooftop of Africa.

The descent was difficult for various reasons. My breathing got better as we skied our way through the scree and boulders to lower altitude, but I had no more water and my energy snacks were long gone. I was very weak and had to stop to recharge frequently. My thighs burned and my body was like a jellyfish. Rodman shared the last of his water with me. We hooked arms, and he steadied me through the endless miles of scree. The pain in my spine and toes from arthritis and the pressure of my boots was excruciating. I just didn't care, though, because I was still euphoric from having made it to the top.

I think I was the last person into camp that day. I could barely walk to the chair behind the dining tent. I took off my socks and shoes, which was so painful I shiver at the thought of it. The sensation of the wind on my toes felt like an electric shock to each nerve. Eventually, I soaked my swollen feet in a kettle of water from the kitchen. Others distracted me while we cut strips of pain patches to wrap around each of my red, gnarled, and swollen toes. I wore my trail shoes the rest of the way down the mountain and wince even now at the mere thought of my hiking boots.

Unfortunately, I soon learned that we still had several hours more to hike before we could rest for the night. Eric offered to have me carried down to the next camp, but I said no way—I'd made it this far. I slowly hobbled my way to the next camp. I missed out on the celebratory beer because I was so late into camp, but I could hear how happy everybody was.

I went right to Kristy's tent and saw that her asthma was under control. To hear her story made me realize how lucky she was to be okay. As I headed to my tent for the night I still recall how positively beautiful the night sky was. The stars seemed to sparkle with joy on their indigo canvas. The night was incredibly peaceful. It was the perfect ending to a memorable and satisfying day. We had each achieved the journey of a lifetime.

The morning came all too quickly, but the coffee and cookies were there once again. We packed up and headed out. I had the chance to get to know a few more of my teammates on the way down. I especially enjoyed talking about motherhood, relationships, aspirations, as well as MS. We shared many personal experiences and real-life situations as if we'd been friends since childhood. Another highlight for me.

In retrospect, I wish that I had not been so depleted every day, so that I could have socialized more. I suspect, though, that we have formed a lifelong bond between all of us. We became more like family than we expected.

Even though the mountain took an enormous amount of energy out of me, it was the experience of a lifetime. This adventure renews my belief that we can do anything we set our minds to, even if someone has MS or PD. I can see why Kilimanjaro is the most grossly underestimated of the Seven Summits. It has a juju of its own. I have new respect for altitude, for being human, and for the sense of personal empowerment. The saying that "Life is a journey, not a destination," makes more sense now. I am humbled by the exceptional strength and fortitude of my teammates as I continue to learn more about each of them. Without a doubt, Kilimanjaro will always be more than a mountain to me.

Susie Weber *learned in 1987 that she had MS; and she's convinced that the disease has made her stronger and has motivated her to live life to the fullest...which is exactly what she does daily. Her turn-of-the-century farmhouse in Jackson, Wisconsin overflows with laughter and activity generated by her three awesome children Austin, Rachel and Joshua, her two dogs Macy and Tanzi, and her incredibly supportive husband of 26 years, Terry. Susie also keeps busy with Weber Design Inc., through which her graphic design and illustrations have earned numerous awards and recognitions for her clients worldwide. And, in her "spare" time, she volunteers, trains for half marathons, skis and works on restoring the family's farmhouse. Susie dedicates this chapter to her father, John Hinrichs, who recently passed away due to idiopathic pulmonary fibrosis, and the many individuals who have shown her how to be brave and taught her to believe that everything is possible.*

To contact Susie:susie@susieweber.com, www.susieweber.com, www.morethanamountain.net

101 Mountains

Glenn Amdahl

WHEN I SUFFERED A LEFT SHOULDER INJURY, WITH associated left hand tremors, my doctor eventually sent me to a neurologist. My diagnosis in May 2006 was left-sided Parkinson's disease; I was 53 years old. My wife was afraid and worried, but for several months I mostly ignored the diagnosis. A combination of medications minimized my symptoms, allowing me to take them and forget about having PD.

In 2010, I went to my appointment at a motion disorder clinic in Seattle. In the waiting room, there was a photo album of Dr. Giroux's mountaineering adventures. Later, I learned of a special climb on Mt. Kilimanjaro for people with MS and PD run by the climbing company, Alpine Ascents International (AAI). On this particular trip, there would be medical people going with the team, including Dr. Giroux. My wife, who was with me, said "You should go…" She didn't have to ask me twice.

Alas, the trip was full, but I suggested that a standby list be started. I became #1 on that list. I have climbed mountains since high school but never anything higher than 14,410-foot Mt. Rainier—Kilimanjaro is nearly a mile higher at 19,340 feet. My wife asked me how many mountains I had climbed since first taking mountain school in 1970. "At least one hundred," I said.

Kilimanjaro, Mountain Climb Number 101

Most of the climbers had signed on early enough to have one year to prepare and train. There was also a long, long list of required equipment from AAI that had to be assembled. While I had made some preparations, like getting a passport, the climb did not seem real until I was officially added in February 2011. I made the team with less than five months to train and prepare. I really had to scramble to get all of the required equipment together and get serious about my training schedule. Other medical problems interfered with my training preparations, as I coped with various PD-related problems and symptoms. My wife made the most inspirational comment, "Make the summit or don't come home!" (She was only joking, I think...)

I had done some extra cross-country skiing that winter at Mt. Spokane's ski area but I knew I would need to do more. Also, there were large numbers of expedition and AAI emails that needed to be reviewed. I began using a nearby 1500-foot-high "mountain," named "Beacon Hill," for training (it gets its name from the airport beacon on top). To make my workout more strenuous, I carried a backpack full of water jugs up and down the mountain.

My plans were disrupted on April 20th, when I awoke

to an agony of pain at 4:00 a.m. and found out I had a left-sided kidney stone. At first, the doctors thought that with the right medicines and time, it would pass. But that course of treatment didn't work. The local specialists were rather busy and I wanted treatment as quickly as possible, so I went to a regional hospital equipped with the "Shock Wave" machine. It is supposed to disintegrate any kidney stone with sound waves, allowing the smaller pieces to pass without the need for surgery. Since it has a 95% success rate, I thought it would be just what I needed. The procedure caused some bleeding and bruising, but I soon felt better and assumed it had worked. I resumed my training. Unfortunately, the doc had gone away for a while, causing my follow-up checkup to be delayed and more time to pass.

In May, an x-ray showed the Shock Wave treatment had only been a time-consuming and expensive failure. The next least invasive treatment was to use a procedure where a tube is inserted through the bladder and laser is used to break up the stone. Unfortunately, this procedure could not be scheduled until late in June. This method worked, but required that a long stent be left in place for several days, which caused some pain and bleeding and left me unable to move very well. Finally at the end of June, the stent was taken out and the doctors gave me an okay to go on the climb...with only 10 days remaining!

While my training was incomplete, I did achieve one milestone—a 15-pound weight loss—I hoped it would help me with the climb. Because of all that transpired, my plans to do a 3000-foot climb up Mt. Kit Carson at a local state park never happened. The Parkinson's disease had also given me some other left-side troubles that included irregular walking and left-eye vision problems. There wasn't much that could be done, however, about any of this and no time to worry…there was a mountain that needed to be climbed.

On July 10th, I left Spokane on a Horizon Air Q400 commuter plane and flew to Portland, Oregon. The flight to Amsterdam was on a Delta Airlines A330 Airbus, and the pilot informed us we would stay north of the Arctic Circle and fly over Greenland. There would be no nightfall—we would remain in daylight for the entire flight.

In Amsterdam, I had to go through security again, but this time they wondered what was under my clothes and asked me to remove whatever it was. I said it was a money belt but explained that it was hard to get off. Wrong answer! "Please step aside," they instructed for a more thorough search. They wanted to x-ray the money belt and took it away. By this time I was the only passenger in security, and since the x-ray machine had no load, it stopped automatically. I asked an inspector to return my money belt to me. He apparently didn't know what was going on—my belt was still in the machine. He asked, "Money belt? What money belt?" and I responded that I would not leave without it. Finally, they "found" and returned it to me, at the same time the airport loudspeakers were calling my name for boarding, announcing that I was delaying the flight.

After boarding the KLM 767 heading for Kilimanjaro International Airport, I finally met the friendly face of someone in our climbing group, Lori Schneider, one of our organizers and our "lead Sherpa." By the end of that day, I had crossed 10 time zones and flown almost 12,000 miles to get to Tanzania. Near the end of the flight, descending through 19,000 feet, I watched the flight info display the outside temperature. Near the summit altitude, it was about 21 degrees Fahrenheit and likely to become colder overnight.

Landing at Kilimanjaro International at night, there was a long delay through customs. At the baggage claim, however, there were lots of locals to help us push carts or carry anything we wished to offload...lots of faces wanting to help...lots of faces wanting us to go with them. Their offers of help felt overwhelming, especially because we'd arrived at nighttime and it didn't feel safe. For the following two weeks, the safest thing any of us could do was stay with our group, guide, or jeep driver.

At the Arusha Hotel, it was time to rest and try to get organized. I emailed my wife that I was "not voted off the mountain yet," so she'd know I was okay. AAI had all the climbers bring their gear to a large conference room for the required "gear check"—every item on their list had to be produced; otherwise, any of us without the required items would not be permitted to go on the climb. It looked like a huge rummage sale as they sifted through everyone's belongings.

I have always liked the safari style clothes with lots of pockets, which any mountaineer can tell you is perfectly in style in any circumstance. For Africa, I came well equipped with multiple sets of safari style shirts, pants, and hat. Okay, okay...truth is, the "fashion police" have been after me for years but to no avail. In downtown Arusha, the local street vendors liked my safari clothes and called to me, "Hey Hollywood!" Finally, I got the proper respect and appreciation I deserved!

Our large group of climbers numbered 28 Americans, 1 European, 2 AAI guides, and 129 Tanzanian porters and guides, a total of 160 people in just our group! I liked the Tanzanian guides—they were very friendly and knew English pretty well. The team spent five days hiking and climbing around the mountain at 12,000-16,500 feet to acclimatize. Including summit day and going back down, the total trek was about 40 miles.

The porters carried amazing loads—most of the climbers' gear, all of their own, plus food, water, tents, portable toilets, a large mess tent, tables, chairs, and more—up and down steep trails and rocky slopes. On the day-after-day trek around Kilimanjaro, and with the other groups on the mountain, it sometimes looked like a Cecil B. DeMille epic trek, with people spanning the trail and porters carrying large loads on their heads as we all made our way down the last ridge, across the valley, and up the next ridge, for as far as we could see.

The evening before summit day, our high camp was at 16,500 feet, but Alpine only allowed us a few hours of sleep before getting us up at 10:00 p.m. They wanted us on the summit by 10:30 a.m. at the latest. Wearing insulated climbing gear and snuggled up in my goose-down sleeping bag, I was sleeping quite well and felt extremely comfortable. *What? Get up now and climb in the cold and dark?* I'm sleeping and comfy...go away, I thought! Slowly coming around, I remembered...*Oh yeah; this is summit day on Mt. Kilimanjaro...this is why I'm here!*

There is no organized rescue from Kilimanjaro—no helicopters, no mountain rescue team from the park service or army. Sick or injured climbers must either walk out on their own, get carried out by their team, or receive help from other climbing groups, if possible. Third-world type medical help could be a few days away, with treatment uncertain. These risks are typical for remote high altitude climbs, and in deciding to climb, each climber has to assume them.

I had discussed the risks with my wife prior to the trip and knew what I would be facing. Kilimanjaro is mostly an altitude and endurance test. When climbers fail on this mountain, it is usually because they try to go too high too fast and get altitude sickness. Some fatalities are due to falls, but most are related to exposure, in cold and bad weather. Our route on Kilimanjaro would give us five days to acclimatize for altitude, and the anticipated weather did not look extreme. In the event of any serious medical problem, I thought the best plan would be to get back to Europe. The most significant thing about our team was that we were doing this summit with 14 "impaired" climbers.

After climbing for a couple of hours, somewhere above 17,000 feet, in the dark, cold, and windy conditions, I found that I was not very steady. Because I was having some trouble, I stayed focused on not falling down. Lack of sleep, excessive exertion, and higher altitude were causing me, on occasion, to doze off or blackout for a second or so—it made me wobble more and was very disturbing. If

I passed out, I suspected they would most likely give me oxygen and send me back down. There was no way I was going down, so I did everything possible to stay awake and keep moving.

If any of us went up too fast, we could become light-headed and dizzy, so the guides often repeated *polé polé* in Swahili, which meant "slow, slow." Hour after hour, we were reminded. I coped with being unsteady by focusing on regular breathing, going slow, and by "double poling" forward and uphill with both trekking poles as I moved my feet using the "rest step" method. This technique of regular, timed climbing and breathing allowed me to keep going for hours.

Even though I had six layers on and was working hard to go uphill, I was getting colder as I climbed. It was clear that I was pushing myself—maybe even too hard. On a mountain with bad weather and dangerous climbing, I might have turned around so as not to endanger others. With Kilimanjaro, however, even though this mountain was cold and high, I knew it wasn't too dangerous. Besides…a sunny day was coming. With a slow, steady pace, the summit was definitely possible.

On earlier trekking days, extra stops had been made to let porters pass, but not today. I required extra unscheduled stops because of both my recent stent and the amount of water they instructed us to drink to counter altitude effects. On summit day, however, Ben from Alpine didn't want me to continue stopping—he asked that I try to keep going. At one point he checked in to see how I was doing. "A little wobbly, but I'm staying with you," I replied. Alpine had split our group into three smaller groups according to climbing speed: slow, medium, or fast. With some groups passing and various other groups in the area—it was impossible to know in the dark where everybody from Alpine was or how they were doing.

My wife had inspired me by saying, "Make the summit or don't come home." I knew she had only been joking but her ultimatum gave me another reason to carry on. Alpine gave us an absolute turnaround time of 10:30 a.m., whether or not we had made it to the summit. Finally, we arrived at Stella Point, on the crater rim, at about 6:00 a.m., just before sunrise. Our leader Eric was there to offer the last of some coffee and his congratulations. After Stella Point, the uphill angle was much less. Since sunrise was coming soon, headlights went out. It looked like an easy couple miles uphill to the summit.

I made the summit at 19,340 feet, the highest mountain in Africa, at approximately 7:30 a.m. Ben took my picture by the famous Kilimanjaro summit sign just a few seconds before another group of climbers crowded around it. My face was sort of frozen despite the balaclava, wool cap, and two hoods. Later, Ben seemed concerned about the time our group had spent in the cold and said, "We need to start getting these people off the summit." So, down we went, for the rest of that day and the next. Just enough time to say, "Goodbye fabulous Kilimanjaro, we'll never forget you!"

If you ever read Hemingway's well-known story, *Snows of Kilimanjaro*, it might seem good to avoid cuts, scrapes, and infections in Africa. On the many trekking days, crossing rocky or steep sections, and on the extra-long summit day, I managed not to fall down, that is, until our return to High Camp.

Tents were set close together with tent lines all around (the guys called them "trip wires"). Tripping on one gave me a good scrape on one hand. I cleaned it up with alcohol wipes and a bandage, and then our camp moved down the mountain and I didn't check it again until evening. When I took a look that night, there were red and blue streaks spreading from the remaining ground-in specks, so I decided to visit the team doctor. Tweezers from the AAI first aid kit and a proper cleaning and bandaging by Eric of AAI took care of the problem, but it was interesting to realize how fast this could have become something much more serious. In Hemingway's story, a minor scratch on the leg from a thorn bush, not properly tended, resulted in gangrene infection. Eric said, "If this is our worst injury on this trip, we did really great, as compared to what it could have been."

Most of us spent a few days on a safari of the famous wildlife parks in Tanzania, the Tarangire National Park, Ngorongoro Crater Conservation Area, and Serengeti National Park. At Tarangire, we had driven only a minute or two into the park when we began to see the most amazing sights. And it went on throughout the entire day. Animals of all sorts, some with young…herds of elephants, giraffes, wildebeests, water buffalo, zebra, gazelles…also vultures, monkeys, baboons, warthogs, and deer. On the crater rim of Ngorongoro, a large lioness stood almost invisible only a yard or so off the road. I knew the security escorts at our nearby lodge were there for good reason.

We had not seen any rhinos in the three national parks we'd visited—many have been lost to poachers. On the last day of our jeep safari, two hours before sunset in the Serengeti, I challenged our driver, Carlos, saying, "find us a rhino." He drove for a while and pointed at grey round rocks in the distance. Was it a rock or a rhino? We weren't sure. We drove on, and then he found one! A large rhino with a big horn, still far away, but clearly visible through my binoculars. Carlos radioed the other jeeps, saying in Swahili that he'd found a rhino. They replied, "You liar, you didn't find one," but they came anyway to see for themselves.

On our last day in Tanzania, our adventure was concluded with an early morning, hour-long hot air balloon ride across the Serengeti Plain. For a long distance, our balloon floated alongside a small river, where many groups of hippos were gathered. Later we looked straight down to see cheetahs chasing gazelles in every direction. Our balloon pilot delighted in bringing us directly into a tree, then lifted the balloon at the last second to clear it. He said this was why so many trees have flat tops in Africa. Some trees held nests of baby vultures or other birds at the top. The pilot asked if we should bump into another nearby balloon. "NO!!!" we said in unison as the balloon bumped...nothing happened. Someone asked how long he had piloted hot air balloons. "This is my first day," he replied jokingly.

The trip home had six flight segments. I jumped back through ten time zones in the other direction. Sleeping at home, I experienced what some refer to as "re-entry." When I'd wake in the morning, I'd be back in Africa, ready to pull on my boots and climb into the jeep for the day. Sometimes, I'd momentarily think it was time to get ready for the climb or for the porters to come and bring morning coffee to my tent. When I mentioned to my wife how great it had been to have porters bring coffee to my bedside first thing in the morning, she said, "Well…you should have brought them home with you!"

My thoughts and dreams lingered in Africa. I hope to find reasons to visit it again. Mt. Kilimanjaro is not the highest or the hardest mountain in the world, but it is famous, and rightly so, one of the "Seven Summits." I offer many thanks to AAI, to all the members of our Mt. K team, and to our Tanzanian porters and guides who made this climb possible and very special. To have climbed one of the Seven Summits was a dream come true and very worthwhile to me—even if I never get to climb the remaining six.

Glenn Amdahl is a computer scientist and has worked for years in aerospace in Seattle, Washington and San Pedro, California. He has a BS degree in computer science from Washington State University. He now lives in his hometown of Spokane, Washington with his wife, Heidi, two daughters, two toy poodles, two cats and two rabbits. When not mountain climbing, you might find Glenn out sailing, skiing, bicycling, canyoneering or traveling with the family. His email is gamdahl@cet.com.

High on Humor

"Comedy is simply a funny way
of being serious."
- Peter Ustinov

Your Mountain is Waiting

Kristy Banaszak

PREPARE TO BE SHOCKED: BEFORE KILI, I WAS A newbie to this whole mountain climbing business. Though some may believe this petite, middle-aged body was built to scale the Barranco Wall, my knees screamed otherwise. Unfortunately, somewhere between raising kids and working full-time, my lifelong dream of climbing Mount Kilimanjaro had fallen by the wayside. But when I first received Lori Schneider's email about the trip, my teenage self that had once been obsessed with the mountain was reawakened. The thought of viewing this fascinating mountain firsthand, instead of in the pages of a magazine, was irresistible. I spent the next year secretly working to find a way to make my dream come to life at last.

After I finally shared the details with my family, reality set in. Aside from the financial implications this trip would have for us, I was quickly overwhelmed by my rigorous training schedule and the massive preparations required. I knew I couldn't do this alone. For the first time since I had been diagnosed in 2005, I had to open up to others about my multiple sclerosis. Church members and friends were somewhat aware of my condition, but my fellow coworkers had no idea. Disclosing one of my greatest insecurities in the workplace was a big step for me, but I understood that I would truly need their support. I dreaded the thought, however, that they would look at me in a different way or see me as "sick." It took some courage, but I now realize that the help I received from them benefited me greatly. I appreciated their warm acceptance.

Although I knew my coworkers, friends, and family meant well, some could not hide their surprise at hearing that I was taking on such an impressive challenge. Some of the most amusing responses included: "Don't take this the wrong way, but you don't look like a mountain climber." "You? Climb a mountain? I've always considered you weak." "Kilimanjaro? That's not in the U.S." And my favorite comment: "Is it really a good idea for a bunch of tired people to climb a mountain?" With all this encouragement, I knew I had to do it. This fatigued, asthmatic woman was about to claim her mountain.

The one person who never doubted me for a moment was my mother, Alice. She witnessed and participated in the growth of this dream of a lifetime. When I described the trip to her and she saw my passion, my mom needed no more convincing to be certain that I could achieve this goal. In fact, her passion nearly matched mine as she threw herself into the preparations for this adventure. She spent nearly as many hours researching as she did shopping for me. Almost daily, she sent emails with updates on her discoveries.

Every few weeks I received another package in the mail containing important supplies for the climb. One of the most essential yet often overlooked items I received from her was the nifty bra purse. *Where else would I keep my lipstick and mascara while climbing the tallest mountain on the continent of Africa?*

As I focused on getting my body into shape, my mom continued to practice her super-shopper skills. Thinking about how to ensure that all my personal hygiene needs were met, she purchased several brands of "dry shampoo" and tested them out to determine which would be most effective. After all, she didn't want me halfway up the mountain only to discover my dry shampoo had left my hair dull and limp. My mother most definitely offered a lightness of spirit to this intense undertaking.

Of course, I can't forget to mention some of my other unexpected pre-trip adventures, thanks to her involvement. One day, a small package arrived. Even after I unwrapped it, I still could not recognize the foreign object I was holding. Once I'd properly identified the "pee funnel," all that was left to do was practice. I won't go into the details, but after weeks of rehearsal at home, I was still unable to successfully utilize the device on the mountain.

Although some of the gadgets my mother sent were strange, I realize that I never could have been so well prepared for this trip without her expert packing skills. The week before my scheduled departure, she traveled six hours to wrap, bundle, and bag all my supplies, from thermal socks to my daily snacks. As a special surprise, she had each member of my family include a note in every snack baggy. When I found the first note on Day One of the climb, my daughter's words of love and encouragement brought tears to my eyes. Every day I eagerly anticipated a little glimpse of home and was reminded of the loved ones who were cheering me on from 8,000 miles away.

The year of planning and training turned out to be more fun than I had expected. To further prepare my body for this rigorous endeavor, I signed up for 10 weeks with a personal trainer. The agonizing lunges and squats helped prepare me for the rocky climb. My friend Susie was also signed up for the trip, so we were able to share our excitement as well as our fears. Susie and I knew that the altitude on Kili might be a challenge, so part of our training was devoted to attacking the highest point in our county, the second highest point in Wisconsin. We hiked the trail at Pike Lake State Park up to the Powder Hill lookout tower, elevation 1,350 feet. Then we ran up and down the 55-foot high tower stairs as many times as we could endure before hiking back down the trail. Exhausted and sweating, we could only hope that our hard work would make us *somewhat prepared* for Kili's daunting 19,340-foot peak.

From the moment the plane touched down in Arusha, I could not contain my amazement that I was about to fulfill my lifelong dream. I felt so privileged to be included in this group of incredible individuals. Each person on this trip had a significant impact on me, and I made lasting friendships with many of the climbers. I never imagined that such a strong bond would form between a group of people who had been strangers previously. I treasure the memories of my conversations with the many climbers, including those with MS and their companions. It was a very special setting to be in, hearing about the challenges and triumphs the other climbers had experienced in their lives as we made our way along the rough terrain of Kili together. Listening to stories of enduring the pain over the loss of a loved one, the fear of the unknown, the struggle of dealing with chronic pain, the disappointment of a lost relationship, and even the challenge to a person's faith, filled me with pride to be part of this courageous group. These people struggling up the mountain were facing the challenges in their personal lives head-on. Not only that, these wonderful people had room in their hearts to nurture fellow climbers. It was truly a privilege and an honor to be part of this amazing group of people.

My companion climber, Connie, served as a wonderful inspiration to me as well. Her previous climbing experience and her warm personality made her the perfect companion. Connie helped get me out of the tent each morning and pushed me through my tedious morning routine. Much like at home, I found myself spending far too much time getting ready in the morning, but Connie helped me break those old habits. She laughed when she saw me painstakingly roll up my sleeping bag on the first morning. Connie grabbed my sleeping bag and showed me how to quickly stuff it into its sack. She tossed my gear into my boundary bag while I struggled to lace up my boots. During the climb, Connie gave me helpful tips on how to use my poles. I could not have asked for a more patient and understanding partner.

My native guide, Mathew, also supported me every step of the way. His smiling face was the first site to greet me each morning as I stepped out of my tent. Every day, Mathew enthusiastically handed me my bagged lunch and said, "Don't forget your lunch, my dear." He sang Tanzanian songs to cheer me up when the climb was most strenuous, and he even held my hand during the steepest parts of our ascent.

At 18,700 feet—only about 600 feet from the summit—I experienced respiratory distress due to my asthma. Lori knew I was in trouble, and I was forced to turn my back on the summit. Mathew put his arm around me, called for another guide to assist, and the two of them hurried me back to High Camp. I have little memory of the panicked trek down and my revival at camp, but I will never forget Mathew's kindness when I was most helpless. Once we reached camp, Mathew gently set me in my tent with my dusty feet outside, took off my gaiters, and unlaced my boots. He then ran to ask another member of our group for help. He said, "Kristy is in trouble! Come!" I was fortunate to have such a caring guide.

Some people have asked me if I feel like I failed. I can honestly say that even though I did not reach the summit, I accomplished more than I ever thought was possible. And I achieved a dream of a lifetime. In the process, I've never been more dust-covered, greasy-haired, and completely exhausted than I was on that mountain. I'm proud of the dirt that I spent weeks removing from underneath my fingernails. I'm proud of each step I took, even when it took every ounce of effort to put one foot in front of the other. I'm proud that I could even make jokes when some members of our group were ready to collapse. I'm proud that after never before climbing above 1,500 feet, I managed to climb to over 18,000! I'm even proud of the three toenails I lost along the way! Believe me, I am not Wonder Woman. Climbing Kilimanjaro was one of the most difficult things I have ever done, but I did it! And I am proud to have been able to cross this feat off my bucket list.

I consider myself to be an average person; I just happen to have MS. I'm a wife and a mother, a church organist, and I have a passion for mystery novels and crossword puzzles. I once believed that MS would limit my ability to take a risk or have an adventure. After all, at times when I have been barely able to make it through a full day of work without wanting to nap, how could I have imagined being able to cross the world and climb a mountain? As I found out, though, MS was not an end of a dream but a path to fulfilling one. This trip renewed my self-confidence, and I know that with the help of my Lord, there are no struggles I cannot overcome.

One of my goals is to share this experience with others. I hope that my accomplishment will be a source of encouragement to those who are facing challenges in their lives. Everyone has mountains to climb. And everyone's mountain is different. Mine just happened to be in Africa. Today is *your* day; your mountain is waiting.

Kristy Banaszak lives in Jackson, Wisconsin with her husband, two children and their cat. She is currently working at an insurance brokerage assisting clients with their employee benefits. Kristy graduated with a degree in elementary education and also studied music in college. Although she is no longer in the education profession, Kristy enjoys teaching in the youth ministry of her congregation and plays organ occasionally for her church. Kristy loves listening to the beautiful violin and cello music performed by her talented children. Her daughter, Kaila, is a sophomore at Carthage College in Kenosha. Her son, Seth, is a senior at Kettle Moraine Lutheran High School in Jackson. Every day seems to bring a new adventure, even if it's just getting groceries. In addition to working and grocery shopping, Kristy enjoys napping with her adorable cat, Alex. Kristy's next big adventure will be the Wisconsin Bike MS: Best Dam Bike Ride 2013. She is looking forward to celebrating the 30th anniversary of this famous ride with her husband, Tom.

Mt. Kilimanjaro, Parkinson's Conquers the Top of Africa

John Carlin

JULY 18, 2011

It took us 6 hours and 25 minutes to get to the summit from High Camp (15,500 feet). Now, we are waiting for the sunrise. A small, reddish-orange orb appears on the horizon. Then, all of a sudden, bang! Two lines shoot out horizontally from the sun, as if they are resting on the clouds. It is a sight to see.

We are 19,340 feet (5895 meters) above sea level at a point called Uhuru Peak. It has taken us six days of hiking to get to High Camp. Acclimating has been the name of the game. In what seems like another lifetime, we have gotten this far with an amazing group of hikers and our leader Lori Schneider who—after being diagnosed with MS—climbed the Seven Summits of the world.

This will be Lori's second time reaching the summit on Kilimanjaro. Her companion is her 79-year-old father. Lori's credo "Empowerment Through Adventure" is very evident throughout our group—our band of Differently Abled Adventurers—four with PD, ten with MS, two Alpine Ascent guides, and fourteen healthy climbing companions who have volunteered to go on this journey, along with a smiling band of porters.

I and my wife and climbing companion, Martha, had the good fortune to reach the summit first out of our group of 28, of which 21 will make the summit. All of the PD climbers made the summit; each coming from different geographical areas around the U.S. With determination to reach it, creativity had been added to each person's training schedule at home as compensation for the various altitudes we've all come from. Some live a blip above sea level. Others, a few more feet up—in places such as Michigan, Wisconsin, Atlanta, Oregon, Washington, Wyoming, and even Spain, to name a few. My wife and I live more than a mile above sea level—we are from Colorado.

As we stand atop Africa, on Uhuru Peak, it's just past sunrise. Martha turns to me and says, "You know, never in my wildest dreams would I have ever thought nine years ago, when you were diagnosed with PD, that one day we would be standing on top of Kilimanjaro." We turned toward each other with tears in our eyes and then kissed and hugged. Not to break the mood of the moment, however, Martha gives me the universal sign for, "I am freezing my tookess off," and "Can we go down NOW?" So, after 25 minutes on top, we tell Auguste, our guide from Day One, that it is time for us to go down.

En route, we pass our fellow adventurers, cheering them on, giving hugs, words of encouragement, and back slaps, knowing that they will be up there next. A little fluid builds up in my eyes at the sight of our comrades—they make me proud to be a part of this group. This crew of diverse individuals is almost overwhelming to consider when I think of all the different backgrounds from which they have come and the hurdles each one has faced to be here.

As Martha and I began our descent, I thought about what we had done to prepare for this adventure. Our training for this climb had included an added twist in our favor—our starting point gave us a boost; we live at 6,300 feet. We are also blessed to have 54 mountains over 14,000 feet tall, called 14ers, in Colorado. After we were invited to go on this adventure, my first comment was, "We'll get four to five 14ers in easily before we go." At least, that is what Martha and I thought in December of 2010. That year, however, our high country accumulated 230% of normal snow pack. In laymen's terms, that is a butt-load of snow! Because of this, the high country and its 14ers were pretty much closed to hiking, open only to technical snow and ice climbing. This ruled out "14er training" till later in the season. In fact, we didn't get to climb any 14ers until two weeks before we left for East Africa.

With the July deadline for departure to Africa closing in fast, we quickly did our homework and found some nine-, ten-, and twelve-thousand-foot peaks that would help us tone our legs and lungs for what was to come. We even tackled Red Rock's Amphitheater steps—anything to get in an altitude workout. Did you know there are 23 sets of steps (7-10 steps per set) top to bottom, or *tottom to bop*, if you go the other way! Finally, with two weeks left, we found a couple 14ers that were relatively snow-free. (I know that you can drive up Pikes Peak and Mt. Evans and tick off two more 14ers, but we won't even go there.)

Along with some of our neighbors, Martha and I did a couple of 13ers. We also included being on our feet for four to eight hours at a time as part of our training. We hiked in our trail gear—hiking boots and day packs that would comfortably carry 25-35 pounds—along with the food and water we planned to eat and drink that day. We also included a jacket shell and some other necessary stuff in our packs. All that preparation had been well worth it.

Thinking back to our ascent, I reflected on moments from the climb itself. I can't speak for anyone else, but I figured out that for me anything I wasn't going to use for that day's climb could be put into my boundary bag to be carried up by our porters. For the early morning, I needed gloves, gators, and a baseball cap that helped with the high altitude sun as well as for bad hair days, which grew in frequency as the days wore on. After lunch, some of those things got stowed away. By then, our bodies and the day itself had warmed up.

From the second day, as we hiked, all topics of conversation became fair game for both genders about any subject. Of course, I took full advantage of the lack of Marquis of Queensberry rules on subjects, oftentimes adding a few quick barbs to the topic at hand. I cannot let a verbal opportunity go by without at least a rough attempt at a smile and or a laugh. If you haven't figured it out already, I was the team's resident comedian, well-versed at verbal sword play!

Descending to the next camp after our summit, which eventually brought us to the exit gate, provided a new meaning to the phrase "slip-sliding away." The descent required "skating" down scree fields the size of marbles. We started skating at 18,500 feet and continued downward to almost High Camp (15,500 feet) where we enjoyed a post-summit lunch. We then packed up our gear and continued on to our next overnight camp, which was dubbed "Beer Camp."

As we logged in at the rangers station, the rangers just happened to have 16-oz. bottles of Coke as well as some "God-love-them" Kilimanjaro lager for only 5,000 shillings. A steal in any part of Tanzania! Remember, we were still above 12,000 feet at this point. Fortunately, I had the good sense to order more than one. We all formed a circle around our tent and had an impromptu "Happy Hour," Kilimanjaro style, as the Carlins are prone to do. After our Happy Hour, we went off to dinner in the "Big Blue Dining Tent." Eventually, we made our way to our private domiciles and caught up on some well-earned sleep.

"Big Blue" was a creature unto itself. It was our focal point for every meal. It comfortably housed 28 adventurers, 2 guides from Seattle, and our meal porters/ kitchen staff. This baby was BIG! The amazing thing about it was that as large as it was, it was always ready before we got to the next meal, fully set up and waiting for us. Most of the time, it had this red "I Dream of Jeannie" look about it on the inside because of the red inner lining. Meals were a great source of camaraderie and merriment. They were very important for both our nutrition and community-building. This is where we all came together in spirit and in body.

Big Blue was my favorite destination in camp. I knew the whole gang would be there. And that's where we started to become a family. Usually, "the boys" sat at one end—all seven of us. But at any given meal, we'd mix it up with the ladies. It was fun to sit next to someone I didn't know very well. Big Blue was where we got to know each other better, and this is where my sense of community grew. I always enjoyed mealtime because the heart and soul of our group melded together there. You can get to know someone pretty quick when you're staring across the table at them or sitting side-by-side.

Being a quick study, I soon learned on which side of the table to sit. The floor was on an angle for almost every meal. So, unless I wanted to do crunches while I ate my meal, I generally sat on the high side of the table. At least I knew I would fall into my plate instead of falling away from it.

The meals provided by our crew were exceptionally good, especially considering we were above 10,000 feet from almost the get-go. The meals were well-balanced and tasty. For those of us who didn't want whatever was being served, there was always someone who would eat it. We generally had six to eight things to choose from at every meal.

Mealtime was also where I discovered new nicknames for many of our teammates. I was notorious for giving them to people. Take for example Paula. We had been hiking down a canyon one day, and it seemed with every other step she took she ended up falling down. Actually, though, she would land sort of in a modified kneeling position, or the genuflection position that one does in church. For those Catholics among us, you'll totally understand this position. So, I nicknamed her GG, which stands for Genuflection Girl.

Our second guide Ben was renamed "Eye Candy." If I have to explain that nickname, then you'll have to look at our pictures to really appreciate its meaning. We sometimes called our lead guide our "Fearless Leader." One of the girls developed altitude sickness pretty early on. She couldn't keep anything in her, either front or back. She even had problems with water. So one day I went on a quest to find some bananas for her. That was probably the first food she had been able to put down in a couple days. After that, I nicknamed her "Banana Girl" or BG for short.

We also had a neurologist and a physician's assistant on the trip who were referred to as "The Docs." When Sierra first heard Lori speak at the REI in Seattle, Sierra approached her afterward and asked Lori whether she had room to include four PD adventurers on her upcoming trip. Sierra too wanted to be part of this adventure. So, "The Docs" signed up to participate as just two "regular adventurers" joining this special group of people. They hadn't come along to play doctor for everyone. The two of them wanted to be part of the climbing team but basically NOT in the capacity that they ultimately were called to fulfill.

Fortunately or unfortunately, however, their roles changed and they became our guardian angels. They ended up taking on the task of watching over all of us, especially the folks with a compromised system. The only problem was that in this role, the two of them were on 24/7 "mountain time" call—making themselves available any time of day or night as we continued to gain ground and make our ascent up the mountain.

One of the more humorous wellness-related stories was when someone came down with an affliction and Martha pulled out her bag of homeopathic tinctures that took the place of conventional medicine. This bag of homeopathic tinctures eventually led to "Martha's General Store and Homeopathic Remedies." When anyone came down with something, they went over to Martha to see if she had anything for what ailed them. Appointments were usually made around the dinner table, leading to a visit to our hut—I mean tent—that night. As a result of what everyone discovered, and being amazed by how homeopathics work with our systems, Martha had regular clientele daily.

My favorite time on the trail was hiking with the different individuals. Everyone had such an incredible story to tell and they were all real. And everyone with a compromised system, either due to multiple sclerosis or Parkinson's disease, never complained about it. If you had looked at our group, you'd never have known that anyone amongst us was dealing with challenges beyond those we all shared in attempting to climb Kilimanjaro.

Along the way, I had the chance to have conversations with everyone about their disease. The only bitching I ever heard was the kind that related to such things as: "I had stones in my shoes," "Boy, it's getting hot!" "When will this madness end?" or "I can't wait till dinner." I found out about family members, sons, and daughters. I learned what people did for enjoyment and how they had come to be on this trip. We talked about why they had wanted to be on this adventure and what they had done to get in shape for the trip.

These people were amazing. We became like a family, sharing our ups and downs and sideways with each other. We even had an opportunity to hear one of our group sing at 15,000 feet. It was incredible. These guys became like brothers and sisters to me. And the co-climbers amazed me with their incredible selflessness. They had volunteered out of the blue. These co-climbers came in every shape and size you can imagine. I have a special place in my heart for all of them. They will always be near and dear to me. And I know I could pick up with any one of them today, right where we left off when we were last together.

I can never express the honor bestowed upon me to be amongst these folks. These Differently Abled Adventurers will always be with me, hopefully as much figuratively as literally, no matter what course their disease, or mine, heads. It has been such a wonderful experience and an honor to be with these dear friends. I will always remember them, no matter where my journey takes me.

What do I hope you take with you on your journey? First, do not let anybody ever tell you that you're limited in what you can do. Your limitations are only in your brain. Second, find your own Kilimanjaro and conquer it. That may be as simple as being able to swim to the far end of the pool, taking one lap around the high school track, planning a trip to somewhere exotic, or going with a group of people to Rocky Mountain National Park and doing your own thing on the front porch of the Stanley Hotel.

Personally, I have decided that my Parkinson's will never take me down. The bus is going to hit me well before that happens. I look forward to my next adventure with my newfound friends. Wherever our feet may take us, they'll all be with me.

John J. Carlin lives in Parker, Colorado. He is a small business owner and an importer of Aqua Hydration Formula, a homeopathic supplement. John was 52 years old at the time of the Kilimanjaro climb. He is a speaker on "Hope, Health and Humor—Parkinson's Disease," sharing with groups about alternatives to help individuals battle PD. He also enjoys fly fishing, road biking, camping, rock and mountain climbing, hiking, mountaineering, bagging 14ers, the RAGBRAI ride across Iowa, as well as U.S. and international travel. You can contact John at doublehaul3@comcast.net.

What I Learned From Climbing Mount Kili

Suz Thomson

WHEN I RETURNED FROM THIS ADVENTURE, I wondered what I had just learned, what had made the most impact. It became clear to me how so many of life's lessons were set before me and defined on this trip. Lessons we have all learned throughout our lives. Call them common sense or actual God-given lessons. Lessons of growth, lessons on becoming a better, more complete person—the authentic self we are supposed to become as we travel on this wondrous and oftentimes difficult journey through life. The following reflects much of what I've learned thus far. I'm sure as I continue on my life's journey that even more will be revealed. Our time on the mountain has and will continue to enhance all of our lives.

LESSON #1—SHUT UP AND
LISTEN TO THE VOICE INSIDE.

Lesson #1 has been the most valuable lesson of all for me to take into my heart. I actually learned Lesson #1 in 2009 when my friend, Lori Schneider, who had just returned from climbing her 7th summit, EVEREST, told me about her plans for another trip through her foundation, Empowerment Through Adventure. She intended to take a group of people who had MS up Kili and planned to have each person accompanied by a companion. Out of nowhere I said, "I want to be one of the companions." The voice inside was very loud and extremely strong. I walked away wondering where the heck that had come from, as I'd never had any intentions to *ever* climb a mountain.

I had spent years fighting off that voice by trying to control my life the way I saw fit and occasionally hitting a wall and taking a wrong turn along the way. So listening to this voice was a huge step for me. I understood it was my Higher Power, whom I choose to call God, the one who speaks volumes when and if I am willing to listen. That being said, the voice that usually controlled my life, and sometimes referred to me as "Dumb Susan," had to put in her two cents worth as well. *"Really, you are going to climb a mountain? Yah, right. Did you forget you have a fear of heights, and who are you kidding, sleeping in a tent for seven days without a shower? Excuse me, but did you also forget you are the condo queen?"* And my personal favorite, *"You realize Africa has killer spiders the size of Iowa, with very large teeth."* This observation set off a big alarm inside, since I have arachnophobia. I decided to put this voice on a big timeout, and I am happy to report she still is.

So, by August 2010, the trip was in place. After discussing it with my husband (he being the voice of reason and also the check writer), Bryce was 100% behind me. "Suz," he said, "you have to do this." I sent in my bio and deposit and NEVER looked back—and I never felt any doubt.

I finally trusted myself and the power greater than me to do this.

LESSON #2—GO WITH AN OPEN MIND AND DO NOT HAVE EXPECTATIONS.

I made a conscious effort to embrace Lesson #2. I understood that I was going into unknown territory with people I had never met before. That in itself was enough to deal with—and a bit overwhelming. By not having expectations, it freed up the adventure for me in ways I never would have thought possible.

Having an open mind, rather than expectations, allowed me the ability to be in the moment and go in whatever direction I needed at the time. I realized traveling to a third world country, a country whose culture was unlike anything I had ever before experienced, would have unforeseen challenges. I needed to be able to accept delays and to be available for my companions when I was needed. There was no room on this trip for expectations.

LESSON #3—EVERYONE HAS A STORY...

We are all faced with challenges in our lives, some greater than others. I think of my life as the melting pot of emotional pain—some self-inflicted, some not. I have learned many excruciatingly difficult lessons along the way, each one making me stronger. My greatest continual lesson has been the loss of my only child, Dave, in 2003. After his death, I was incapacitated, to say the least. The person I had been while Dave was alive was destroyed and a new persona had to be created. I was left with the daily questions of, *"What is my purpose now? I was Dave's mom, so who will I be beyond that? Do I even want to continue in this life?"*

On this trip it became very clear to me that we all have challenges. Challenges, regardless of what they are, can render us helpless and lost. By stepping out of myself, away from my grief, and in being there for someone else, I took a huge step in my ongoing healing process. This truly was a very valuable lesson for all of us.

LESSON #4—NOW I HAVE A CHOICE TO MAKE.

After Dave's death I had to decide: was I going to take the high road as I climbed out of this huge pothole of life or was I going to remain embedded there? Taking the high road requires a little more work. It requires grabbing hold of the hands that are stretched out to you. Was I willing and able to ask for help? My sister, Beth, has been my ongoing lifeline. She said to me, "Suz, you have to let people help you. They need to. They are hurting also. They want to help." This was a huge lesson. So, with that, I began my climb out towards the light.

Through compassionate friends, counseling, and the love of family and friends, my husband, Bryce, and I slowly made our way out. This is very much like the story my friends with MS and PD shared. They went through grief, their lives were threatened, they had to come to terms with their new life's direction, and they reached out to family and friends much the same way I did. They made a conscious decision to seek medical treatment and find holistic healthful ways to manage their new lives.

As a personal trainer, I was in awe of everyone. They all said exercise was a huge aspect of their new life—it helped their disease immensely. It helped with depression issues as well, and it helped to keep symptoms more manageable. On the mountain, there was never a complaint. They all kept forging ahead regardless of the conditions. Some of them experienced symptoms due to stress and being overtired. My companion's right leg shook, and she had double vision in the evenings because she was so tired. Again, she never complained. She simply demonstrated a quiet acceptance and then rested.

LESSON #5—ONE STEP, ONE DAY AT A TIME.

This is a simple statement we all know only too well, but really, how often do any of us apply this to our daily lives? At dinner the night before we left for the mountain, I mentioned that I was going to take this climb step-by-step. I didn't want to project, and I didn't want to miss a minute of it. Some agreed this would be the best way to approach the mountain.

And it was. Not only did I take it minute-by-minute, but I really didn't want to know what was coming the next day. Nor did the guides tell us. Each day, the climb offered challenges none of us expected. We truly climbed parts of the mountain, hand over hand and feet. I have a fear of heights, but I took charge of myself, and again, a strength I never knew I had within me surfaced. I was exhilarated by this accomplishment. I set fear aside and took it one step at a time, completing that day's challenges with hugs. Every day was a summit day for me. Every day presented a new and exciting challenge. I was getting stronger mentally and physically with each passing day. We all were.

For many of us, the greatest challenge was altitude

sickness. It hit me on the fourth day. I was fortunate because I only experienced nausea, but some suffered from headaches and vomiting. Nasty stuff. Again, one step, one day at a time.

LESSON #6—YOU DO NOT ALWAYS HAVE
TO REACH THE TOP TO BE OR FEEL SUCCESSFUL.

Sometimes you are a winner by just showing up. Everyone on the team, regardless of how high they climbed, was a winner. Everyone's personal goals were met—some were even exceeded.

"I can, I will, I am." We used my personal training mantra throughout our time on the mountain. At the end of the trip, it was evident…*We could, We did, and We are…*

…AND SOME OF THE OTHER STUFF I LEARNED

First, I can act like a grownup for 15 hours of travel time on an airplane. I got up regularly (much to the dismay of the guy in the aisle) because I didn't want to develop any clots. It also kept me from going *a little* nuts.

Second, a person can live without changing their underpants for seven days when they discover they left them in the hotel room. The day we were doing the equipment check, I tucked them away so no one would see the holey undies I'd brought along. I had intended to pitch them out one-by-one at the end of each day. My lack of underwear was brought to my attention when I woke on the first morning in camp and looked for them. My partner Gina thought it was hysterical—me, not so much…

There was always something that started our morning out in a fit of giggles. That is pretty much how we went to sleep at night as well. At the start of each day while we drank our morning coffee, which was delivered to our tents, (did I mention we were spoiled?), Gina whipped off her stocking hat (we slept in them for extra heat) and asked, "Hey Suz, how does my hair look today?" You can imagine the sight before me. We shrieked with laughter. Thankfully, we didn't have any mirrors, but through the wonderful world of photography, some of those less-than-attractive images did get captured on film…

Third, I no longer say, after a day's workout, "Gee, I smell like a boy." I now say, "Oh my goodness, I smell like a porter." (God bless them!) Seriously, we could smell them as they flew by us going up the hill, hauling on their heads or backs the 35 pounds of gear we didn't have in our daypacks. They were billy goats in the flesh. These amazing, wonderful men—from the Chagga tribe that lives at the base of Kilimanjaro—spoke excellent English as well as the Tanzanian native tongue of Swahili. They always had a smile on their faces and a gentle and kind word when we needed it most.

Fourth, you can learn to be creative when it comes to your bathroom needs. The biggest hurdle at night, when I left the tent to seek out the Porta Potty, was to not twist an ankle. I didn't mind these late night interruptions as the night skies were my favorite. I stood in awe under them, wishing I could pluck a star and thanking God for putting me on this journey. Even with the brilliant night sky, however, navigating at night was a challenge.

Fifth, a person can wear the same clothes for seven days, without a shower, and she may just have a meltdown or two along the way. I simply added to my base layer as we gained altitude. I summited wearing three pairs of long underwear, insulated ski pants, my ski jacket, my down jacket, and down mittens. I looked like an Oompa Loompa, yet I was still frozen. The hand warmers only heated up halfway since without oxygen they didn't activate very well.

In the summit picture that was posted, my husband, Bryce, and my sister struggled to guess which one I was. Bryce checked the closet to see that my white jacket was gone and then they both decided I was the big white puffy one—it was my nose and *kind of* my smile that they were looking at...one of the side effects of being oxygen deprived was swelling.

My face had puffed up...and oh, did I mention altitude sickness and lack of oxygen caused me to be crabby? I had a meltdown on the top of the largest free-standing mountain in the world. Good grief! My hands were frozen, and I couldn't make them work to get my camera out of the backpack. My Snickers bar had frozen, and I wasn't about to break a tooth in Africa. I was starving, freezing, and exhausted. Of course, my companion—who had watched this scene evolve—had to say, "My, my, someone is having a *little* meltdown."

On the way up, about midway, we had all struggled. At one point, I laid down on a rock and started to go to sleep. One of our guides came over and said, "Susan, you cannot sleep. You must get up." He gently got me to my feet, and I was able to get an energy gel out of my pocket and ingest it. I then yelled, from out of nowhere, "I can, I will, I am!" I wasn't really sure where that had come from, but I then looked up and saw that the top of the mountain was within reach. We all kept moving forward at that point and there were lots of hugs and tears at the top.

It was kind of frightening for me that I couldn't seem to control my emotions, nor did I like what came out. What I learned from this: When on the mountain, you will not act yourself. Once back at High Camp I mentioned to our photographer Jeff that I planned to pass up journaling the day's activities. He asked why, and I said, "Even I don't want to read the words I would write. I need to clear my head and regroup."

Sixth, while I coped well with the altitude at the start of our climb, my body expressed itself in a very natural healthy way. Belching on the mountain was a favorite pasttime, and I was cheered on loudly, followed by a "Good for you, SUZ! You are acclimating well!" On the third day, at about 13,000 feet, the belching stopped and I got nauseated and felt the effects of altitude. But it had been pretty fun while it lasted…I did share with the group that I had been raised with four brothers and one sister. We had learned to be competitive in many ways…

Seventh, I also learned how important it was to eat plenty and drink lots of fluids. It flushed out the system, so to speak, so we drank four liters a day. I also learned how important it was to keep eating. The mountain used up every ounce of calories we took in. We were hungry and ate every few hours. Our bodies craved vegetables and fruit as well as protein. We all learned on the mountain the true value of fueling our body with proper food—the food our body asked us for, which was a great lesson for all of us.

The meals provided were unbelievable, all created

on a little Coleman cooking stove. We were served on china at a long dining table, which was very civilized (no eating while standing up by the kitchen sink for me.) We were served three meals a day. Breakfast consisted of porridge, scrambled eggs, bacon, and french toast. Lunch was wonderful—sandwiches, Pringles, and fruit. Dinner started with a lovely soup (ginger, pumpkin, and others), accompanying chicken, beef, or pork, potatoes or rice, and lots of steamed veggies. We were always amazed at how when we left in the morning at 8:00 a.m., four hours later the tent was up and ready to serve our lunch somewhere on the trail, and from there, set up again at our evening camping spot. Those wonderful magicians passed us on our trek. It was mind-boggling really, because as we sometimes struggled, those who would create our next dining experience flew by us with huge smiles on their faces and the greeting "Jambo."

Eighth, on safari, I witnessed firsthand the circle of life. I was struck by how the animals worked together to protect themselves from the predators. The zebras and wildebeests traveled together. One has great eyesight, while the other has keen smell. The monkeys shook the trees that had fruit on them. Below the trees we could see impalas, zebras, wildebeests, and birds eating together, with the baboons not far away picking through elephant dung for seeds. Daytime always seemed peaceful, but as we left the park one night at dusk, we could sense and see the nervousness in the animals as they pranced, paced, and circled their young. They waited for nightfall and the predators that would come out. It was amazing. I thought to myself how we had survived the climb in much the same way—each of us looking out for the other.

An example for me personally was when I was faced with my first rock wall and realized that I would be scaling it without guide lines or help. I tensed up. Behind me came encouraging words, "Suz, you can do this. Take your time and go up slowly one hand over the other. You can do this. Oh, and by the way, this is a Class 4 climb you are doing—you rock!" We were always encouraging each other and watching out for each other's safety, in much the same way as what I witnessed in the animal kingdom.

Ninth, and finally, the greatest lesson I learned was from my MS and Parkinson's friends. They taught me that regardless of their limitations, they did not and would not allow anything to slow them down or define them. They lived in the moment, and they chose to challenge their bodies, minds, and souls on this trip. I am a much better person with a greater understanding of their disease as a result of spending time with them.

I also learned what great human character really is. Everyone came with the dream to reach the top, but we learned it wasn't reaching the actual summit that would forever change us. Rather, the journey we took together and the lifelong bond that was created are what we will all continue to carry with us. We came together as a team of 28 strangers who quickly learned the importance of trust and teamwork.

Through this incredible experience, I saw that we must not let the potholes of life define us, but rather, allow the road on which we choose to travel to distinguish us. I went as a companion and came back a changed person. I bonded with incredible people who taught me that regardless of our limitations, we can do it. If we believe it, we can achieve it.

And one more... My final lesson was the gratitude I carry with me daily. I am grateful to God for giving me the voice and for being my guide on this incredible adventure. I am grateful to myself for listening to it and for believing in me enough to see it through. I am blessed; we all are. This climb truly changed my life and my world, and I will be forever grateful.

If you think you can't, you won't. But if you think you can, you will.

Suz Byerly Thomson, age 56, is a public health employee, personal trainer and motivational speaker. She is married to Bryce Thomson and has one son, now deceased. Suz loves the outdoors and prefers to be outside doing something exhilarating, such as running, biking, skiing or swimming. Suz sings professionally with her husband. She has lived in the Polk County, Wisconsin area for 50 years. You can contact Suz at btnsuz@amerytel.net.

Finding Our Way Back

"The wound is the place where the
light enters you."
- Rumi

Alive in the
Present Moment

Brandis Graves

"YOU HAVE MULTIPLE SCLEROSIS" ARE NOT THE four words anyone wants to hear, especially a month before their 30th birthday. But in November, 2009, I was officially diagnosed with this disease. After denial and a second opinion that yielded the same outcome, I had two choices: (1) Do nothing and remain in denial, or (2) Ask to be shown what to do to treat it. I chose the second…

Looking back I think I always knew deep down that the disease was there, but I am grateful for the years I was able to be in denial and prove to myself what I was capable of. After the official diagnosis, I desperately needed something to give me hope for my future. My past accomplishments helped me move forward, but little did I know that other future events would change my life even more profoundly.

I began physical therapy school in the fall of 2001 at the age of 21. PT school was challenging, to say the least, and although I was excited to have been accepted into the program, the pressures of school and other stressors at the time triggered my first episode of multiple sclerosis in the summer of 2002.

As a PT student, I knew how important exercise and diet were for a person, so I decided to take up the activity I always wanted to participate in, running. I found it was a great way for me to relieve stress and improve my fitness level. Additionally, since there wasn't a lot of time for strenuous, time-consuming activities—between my school and work schedules—running seemed to be a good fit.

I had been running for a couple of months when one morning, I awoke with flashing in my eyes, as if someone had flashed a camera in them. The bright flash looked like blinding white spots and would not go away. I had no idea what was happening, so initially, I tried to ignore it. After a few days, it became so bad that I took myself to the ER where an MRI was done. The ER doctor told me he thought I had MS but wasn't completely sure. He said I would need to follow up with a neurologist for further testing and evaluation.

I was devastated and terrified. *I am 22 years old and might have MS? What am I going to do? Will I be able to continue in school?* Being a physical therapy student, I had learned about the neurodegenerative disease known as multiple sclerosis and the terrible effects it can have on a person. These questions and thoughts swirled in my head for days until I met with a neurologist. He explained to me that the MRI showed I had three lesions on my brain. "It could be MS," he said, but he did not give me an official diagnosis.

By this time, the flashing light had gone away, and the residual effect was lost vision in the same area of both eyes. When I looked at someone in the eyes, their nose was completely gone. "Your vision will come back," the neurologist told me. He did not give me the "official diagnosis," as three spots on an MRI scan were not conclusive. "If you get past the five-year mark with no other episodes, you are in the clear," he added. So I prayed every day and read more "power of positive thinking" books than anyone I knew, because I decided it could help. Deep down, though, there was the fear—the what if's that I tried to keep at bay.

The neurologist turned out to be right. Over the course of the next month or two, my vision fully returned and I continued with PT school. I was given some leniency with my studies, as it was difficult to read when part of what I looked at was missing. I had two strange episodes happen during the next year, but they lasted from a couple of hours to a couple of days and then resolved, so I did not seek out medical attention.

Over the course of the next year, I graduated from PT school, moved, started my first job as a physical therapist, and got married, all the while staying mostly asymptomatic but always having those words in my head, " If you get past the five-year mark you are in the clear."

I gradually began to exercise again, but I was scared. *What had caused the initial attack? Was it exercise? Running? Stress? What was really going on?* When these thoughts came into my mind, I pushed them aside and replaced them with positive ones. Deep down I think I always knew *IT* was there, *but I had not been officially diagnosed so I was in the clear, right?*

During the next six years, I moved several times, gaining

experience in many different areas of physical therapy practice. Despite the stress of different jobs, moving, and a marriage that ultimately ended in divorce, I handled it all as best as I could because I knew that stress "could" cause something to happen. Hence, I did my best to manage my stress for fear of the "what if" factor.

In 2009, I got serious about running again. I was very cautious when I started, as I had learned in physical therapy school that strenuous exercise could cause an MS exacerbation, and I knew the last time I'd started running was when my first "episode" occurred. Even though I had not been officially diagnosed I wanted to be careful, so I started out gradually. This gradual progression led to training for and running my first two marathons; all the while the ominous question "Do I have MS?" loomed in the back of my mind. Although the question was still there, I had finally gotten to the point where I did not think about it on a daily basis and was proud for pushing myself to my limits of training.

I ran the Grandma's Marathon in June 2009 and the Twin Cities Marathon in October 2009. The marathons were quite different in the sense that Grandma's was unbearably hot. People were passing out due to heat strokes. It was not unusual for me to overheat, so I knew that no matter what, I had to try and keep cool. The marathon had water and ice stations along the course. The friend I ran with had run several marathons, and he educated me along the way about where to place the ice to cool the body off as quickly as possible.

"Please let me finish the marathon," I prayed, knowing that doing this was pushing my body to its limits. I will be the first to admit that I am not a fast runner, but considering I had not run in high school, and had problems with overheating, along with knowing that I "could trigger something," I was grateful to be running the marathon at all, no matter what my final time turned out to be. I finished in just over 4 hours and 35 minutes. I managed to lose two toenails due to blood blisters and could barely walk, but I had finished!

After a month off, I returned to training for my second marathon, the Twin Cities Marathon. Training for a race in August in Minnesota can be grueling because of the heat and humidity, but somehow I managed to push on. I had one episode while running one day when my right foot began to tingle and go numb. I slapped my toes down on the ground and thought *Oh no, not today, not now* and pushed on. The symptom went away almost immediately. *Was it related to my back or to something else??* The question was there but I did not dwell on it.

October finally arrived and the weather for the marathon was perfect—cool and overcast! As we stood in the corral waiting for the start gun, I could only hope for a better race than in June. As we left the corral and passed the start line, people lined the street to cheer us on. We ran through downtown Minneapolis, on to the Lakes area, across the city to Grand Avenue, with a finish in downtown St. Paul at the Capitol. I felt great during the marathon and afterwards.

I had done it! I had run my first two marathons and finished! For the first time in a long time I was proud of myself for accomplishing what I once thought was not possible simply because I did not have the confidence in myself. I proved myself wrong.

Seven years had passed since the episode in PT school that shocked my world. I again found myself at a critical juncture, with many stressors, including the possibility of changing jobs and moving. I awoke one morning, about a month after the marathon, with blurred vision in my right eye. It felt as if someone had put a film over my right eye. No matter what I did, the film remained. I tried to go to work that day, but the right side of my face felt like it was on fire and my head pounded. Migraine headaches run in my family, so I hoped and prayed that it was a migraine. Deep down, though, I knew "it" was back. I had to leave work early that day and took the following day off.

I had been given some migraine headache medication by a physician I worked with at the hospital. After taking it when I got home from work that first day, I prayed, "Please, God, let me wake up with these symptoms resolved." It didn't work. I knew from my past experience that I would be sent to an ophthalmologist for further examination. I met with one that week, who told me I had dry eyes and prescribed eye drops. Again, as much as I didn't want it to be so, I knew better.

By the weekend, I was at a point where I could not bear it anymore. I called a friend and asked if she could take me to the ER. Because of my memories, I hated acknowledging that I had to go there. All those emotions and feelings of what had happened seven years earlier came rushing back to me, the biggest of which was fear—it was like everything from seven years ago had just happened.

I spent most of the day at the ER where they asked questions and performed an MRI. I did not tell them about my past episode because I wanted any diagnosis to be made with no preconceived notions. The ER doctor looked at the MRI scans and told me I had nothing more than a migraine headache. He instructed me to go home and rest. I was given the name of a neurologist to follow up with regarding treatment for my migraines and sent home. I was so relieved!! My prayers for a negative MRI scan had been answered...until I received a call the next morning.

I had just arrived at Target and was sitting in my car when my phone rang. It was the ER doctor from the day before. "We had a specialist look at your scans last night and he noted some abnormalities. We think you have MS and you should follow up with the neurologist regarding this."

I was in shock. I remember sitting there, turning to my friend, and repeating the ER doctor's words. I cried. I cried for all I thought I had lost. My mind was racing and I thought I *can't have MS! He said the MRI scan was fine last night, how could it have changed? How could he have missed that?* I was so angry, so scared, and so full of fear about what would happen next that I felt frozen. I had found a love of running—so now what? Had my marathons been just a cruel way of teasing me? How could this be? As a physical therapist I had learned that people with MS should avoid strenuous activity to avoid triggering an exacerbation. But I couldn't believe that I had finally reached a point in my life where I was fit and active and had a hobby I enjoyed, only to have it taken away.

I went home that day and cried. I thought I'd lost everything—my ability to run and to lead the active life I had grown accustomed to enjoying. The next six weeks became a blur. I went to my previously scheduled neurology appointment where I did not like how the neurologist delivered the information, so I sought a second opinion. Surely, he would tell me something different!

Unfortunately, he did not, but he delivered it in a way that was easier to handle. "You will need to have a visual evoked response test and a spinal tap for further testing," he said. He also wanted to put me on IV steroids to address the optic neuritis that had been officially diagnosed.

I received the IV steroids at the hospital where I worked. I was embarrassed, ashamed, and worried that everyone would think less of me or, even worse, that they would pity me. I despised the pity look. I knew that people were concerned, and I appreciated their concern more than I could say, but at the same time, I just wanted to be normal.

The day I received my first treatment, my rehab director brought a man in to visit with me. He too had MS and had been diagnosed in his 30's. He was now in his 50's and doing well. He sat with me for over an hour answering questions, listening to my concerns, and witnessing my tears of pain, all the while wanting to help me see I could have hope for the future that at that moment looked so uncertain. The following day, I had a colleague come in and visit and she said a very powerful thing to me that I will never forget. "You ran two marathons and you had this the whole time, Brandis. Think of how strong you are." I did not feel strong, but those words gave me hope at a time when I felt nothing but hopeless.

I completed the tests, and all were conclusive.

"You have MS," the doctor said.

"Can I still run? And will I be on a golf course golfing

when I am 65?" were the first two questions I asked him.

He smiled kindly and said, "Yes, Brandis. Go live your life. Plan your trip to Africa. I think you will do just fine."

His statement was ironic, since when he said it, I thought, *Africa, why would I go to Africa?* That is not on my list of places to visit. Little did I know those words, spoken by him that day, set in motion a chain of events that would continue to change my life.

After that appointment, the neurologist told me about treatments available for those with MS and he recommended I get started on one soon, especially since he believed I had lived with the disease for seven years without any drug therapy. "You have done really well for a long time without treatment, but since you have had a new episode, you need to start a therapy," he said. So, I agreed to start one ASAP.

I will never forget what happened next. I walked out to the front of the treatment room and was standing at his front desk when he came out with what looked like four three-inch-thick binders, each for a different MS medication. He placed them in front of me on the desk. As he laid them down, the sound they made was as if he had just dropped a load of wood from six stories above. I began to sob. I needed to read each one and select which medication I would take as a treatment. *What was happening? Surely this was a dream.*

Over the next several weeks, I tried to process everything that was happening. I needed to give myself daily injections, start vitamin supplementation, and try to figure out how to manage my stress. I also found out that overheating is a bad thing when you have MS. *Did my marathons trigger the exacerbation?* Probably not. Rather, it was more than likely a culmination of things. I found out that everything I had done to prevent overheating in the Grandma's Marathon had been appropriate and very applicable for heat exposure when one has MS.

At the end of December, I returned to work. By that time, my vision had almost completely returned to normal. I had been blessed over the course of those six weeks off to have met a couple of people with MS who were in their 50's and doing very well, so well that I would not have known they had MS if they hadn't told me. While it was very meaningful to have met these individuals, I desperately wanted to meet someone who still led a full and active life, including marathon running despite their diagnosis. I searched the Internet and sought out a mentorship program from the local MS society but found no one. The neurologist told me I could do anything I wanted and still lead a full, active life—as so many do—*but where were they all?*

In February 2010, I was helping to time the American Birkebeiner, North America's largest cross-country ski race, when I learned that it was a fundraiser for the Wisconsin MS Society. I started researching it and found out that a woman named Lori Schneider would be attending. Lori had been diagnosed with MS and told she would be in a wheelchair within a year after her diagnosis. Instead, she went on to be the first woman with MS to summit all Seven Summits. I read that she would be speaking at the Birkie and I thought, "Here is my hope."

As it turned out, I was unable to hear her speak at the event, so I took a leap of faith and emailed her, asking if she had any of her presentations available for online viewing.

I told her about my story and recent diagnosis and hoped that she would not consider me crazy for contacting her, asking her for inspiration.

To my surprise, I received one of the most heartfelt and genuine emails I have ever had the pleasure of receiving. Lori's email read as if she were reading my mind, my thoughts, and my emotions. I had been feeling alone and lost, and she understood. She emailed me a link to her presentation and also said she was putting together a climb that would consist of individuals with MS. She wondered if I would be interested. The climb would be of Mount Kilimanjaro in Africa, and she thought that because I'd been so active, I would be an asset to the climb. "Yes! Of course, I am interested. Please add me to your list," I emailed back as fast I could.

Over the next several months, I continued to go through the motions of life. I had many nights when I sat home and cried. Maybe because of fear, maybe because of anger from the diagnosis, or maybe because of the pain and welts that came with my injections. There was a lot of trial and error with how to give myself injections. I was so angry! I wondered whether this was what life was going to be like—full of fear, disappointment, and embarrassment. After a while, I began to wonder if this would be my new way of living, trying to accept that this was how it would be. I knew that I was one of the fortunate ones with minimal symptoms, yet I continued to feel devastated. Those four words, "You have multiple sclerosis" haunted me.

Several months later, I heard back from Lori that the trip to Kilimanjaro was officially a go. I was so excited to have something to look forward to, something to challenge myself with, and most especially, that other people who had MS were going to do this as well.

That summer, as I started to train for the climb, I ran my first half marathon in sweltering heat. I cried as I crossed the finish. It wasn't a marathon, but I had proven to myself that I could still run. Although scared out of my mind over the "what if's," I had done it!

In October, 2010, I officially began to train specifically for the Kilimanjaro climb. Initially, I started with snowshoeing and climbing the hills at a local golf course in the snow. I wore my hiking boots and put on my pack, starting with five pounds. As I got stronger, I increased the weight in my pack until by summer 2011, it was up to thirty pounds and I was hiking up and down the local ski hills. My training also consisted of weight training, stair steppers, and of course, some running. I was beginning to push myself physically and mentally again, as part of training is overcoming the mental game of "Can I do this?"

Lori sent out monthly updates regarding where we should be with our training, along with suggestions for training techniques, gear lists, and fundraising ideas—a plethora of information that consistently arrived. Emails began to circulate between climbers and we were introduced to our climbing companion, the person who would climb with us and help us with reminders for medications and be our support and go-to person.

I have to be honest. Initially, I did not care for this idea because I felt it meant that somehow I was weak and needed someone else to help me on the climb. What I found out though was that our climbing partners were just that, a partner for us as much as we were for them—

diagnosis or not—and for that I am forever grateful to have had my partner Patti.

I took everything day-by-day as we got closer to our departure date—the vaccines, the training, and purchasing gear. The trip arrived before I knew it, and suddenly I was packing a boundary bag with gear I had never before used and some I had not even known about prior to the trip.

July 10, 2011 arrived, and as I waited in the Minneapolis airport for my first flight I had a sense of calm about me. I had no expectations for this trip. I really had no idea *what* to expect. Through each leg of the flight I began to meet my fellow climbers, and although I did have one moment of brief panic when I realized I really knew no one and was going to climb a mountain, it quickly passed.

I had never met a group of people that I bonded with so quickly and trusted so easily. I think each of us had our own personal goal, but common goals also brought us closer together—to climb Kilimanjaro and to change the perceptions of others faced with a disease.

The climb began on July 12, 2011 and was the most difficult, rewarding, and meaningful thing I have ever done. I became sick with acute mountain sickness the second night on the mountain and continued to be unable to eat or drink the amount needed to replenish the 4,000 calories burned on the mountain each day or to satisfy the 3-5 liters of water needed for hydration. I vomited frequently and the nausea was unlike anything I have experienced before. *And yet I kept climbing!*

We climbed through five ecological zones of differing terrain—all very steep and dry. I was not prepared for the amount of dust we breathed in on a daily basis. Barranco

Wall (also known as Breakfast Wall since many lose their breakfast climbing it) was the closest thing to vertical rock climbing I have ever encountered…and I loved every minute of it! I was finding an inner strength that I never knew I had. This, I had not expected.

Summit night arrived after five days of strenuous climbing and three days of acute mountain sickness. During the three hours prior to leaving for summit (the night of Day Five) when we were supposed to be sleeping, I was once again vomiting. Knowing that I had made it this far, I told myself that no matter what, I would try for the summit.

I truly thought I could make it, but on the summit attempt, my body let me know that it had been pushed to its limit. I had depleted all of my energy reserves over the prior three days and had been unable to replenish them. I continued to be extremely nauseous and dizziness set in. I could barely stand. I sat on a rock, and one of the guides told me I needed an IV in my arm because I was so obviously dehydrated at that point.

I had done everything I could. I had tried to eat and drink sufficiently, took Diamox for acute mountain sickness, breathed with the correct technique—even with a step, stop, breathe, repeat pattern. Yet, the world began to spin and I needed to rest. I sat on a rock and was offered the very last option. I could administer a suppository to fight the nausea that was debilitating me at that point. I agreed to do it, and after fifteen minutes, began to climb again. However, I began to have diarrhea, at which point I knew I could no longer continue. I had nothing left in my body to draw from and still had more than six hours of climbing in order to reach the summit. I could barely stand, so with swift action, our Tanzanian guide helped carry me down to High Camp where I was assisted into my tent to rest.

I remember coming down from the summit attempt sobbing, "I've failed!" I had come so far and pushed so hard, but my body said, "Not this time, Brandis." For the first time on the trip, I felt ashamed. *How could I not summit?* I asked myself. As I lay in my tent, I dozed in and out of wakefulness. At one point, I needed to get out of the tent to use the tent toilets that had been set up by our Tanzanian guides, and as I returned to my tent, I looked up at the summit.

The moon reflected its radiant glow on the glaciers, and along the route I could see the tiniest of headlamps of the other climbers making their way to the summit. As I took in this beautiful sight I listened to the silence. I prayed a few words for the climbers and in that moment I felt peace. I knew I had not failed. Rather, I had succeeded in something I had not even dreamt of trying one year earlier.

When you climb a mountain, you must remain focused on the present moment. Thoughts and questions such as, *"Where am I going to put my right foot so I can reach across and grab with my left hand?"* while climbing keep you there. I was constantly processing that present moment and found that there was something very freeing about it. Suddenly all the fears, worries, and concerns that had at times been all-consuming during the past year and a half were gone. A weight had been lifted, an empty gap filled, and fear released. I was accepted 100% for who I was, and for the first time in a long time, I was not ashamed. In that moment, I was proud of my accomplishment. For the first time in over a year, I felt alive.

Brandis Graves *grew up on a dairy farm in South Dakota, where she spent much of her time in the outdoors. After graduating with her Master of Physical Therapy degree, she realized her love for travel and outdoor activity, which led her on trips to Guatemala, Belize, England, and Africa. She also became a two-time marathon finisher. Following the Leap of Faith Kilimanjaro climb, Brandis was inspired to explore the mountains and the waters of the Pacific Northwest, where she now resides. When Brandis is not working at a private outpatient physical therapy clinic, she can be found spending time with her fiancé in Washington, enjoying hiking, scuba diving, skiing, and mountain biking. You can follow her adventures at brandisgraves.blogspot. com.*

Breathe In,
Breathe Out

Sarah Conrad

JULY 18TH, 2011 -
Summit day on Mt. Kilimanjaro – 1 a.m.

Deep breath in. Air flooding every cavity. Abdomen and chest straining against hip and chest straps. Forceful, audible exhale. *Repeat.* Five hours of breathe in, breathe out. One foot in front of the other. *Breathe.*

Darkness enveloped the mountain and our small group. Only a snakelike trail of headlamps interrupted the pitch-black slope. Some lights ranged above our position, but most lingered below. The only sound for hours had been my breath and the soft crunch of gravel below my feet. But then, out of the dark, singing erupted. The song bounced among the African guides. Some taking it up as others finished. Others joining in as a round. *"Jambo! Jambo bwana! Habari gani. Mzuri Sana…Kilimanjaro Hakuna Matata."* And then, as we moved farther ahead from the other groups, silence. Only *breathe in and breathe out.*

Each step took me one step closer, but would it be enough? Would I reach the summit or would MS stop me? I knew I was physically fit enough to make it. The two unknowns were altitude and MS. So far altitude hadn't been a problem, but MS had always been a fickle sidekick.

The only symptom I worried about before coming here would finally be put to the test. Would my feet spasm? They always did in the cold. And it was cold—around zero degrees Fahrenheit. I wore the warmest boots and wool socks I could find, but the cold still seeped through. Once the cramps started, they would be nearly impossible to stop.

The previous December, I remember walking around Strasbourg, France, admiring Christmas markets one Saturday evening. It wasn't too cold, perhaps around freezing, but my feet went into spasms to the point I couldn't walk. Starting in the toes, the cramps moved quickly to the arches and finally the calves. The only reliable solution I've found is to get into a warm place and stretch them until the spasms release. That can take up to 30 minutes. Unlike in Strasbourg, there were no warm, inviting buildings to slip into. Only the cold, dark slopes of Africa's tallest mountain.

About halfway into our summit push, the cramps began.

May 12, 2010 –
Brigham and Women's Hospital

A neurologist, six interns, and a social worker gathered in a semi-circle at the foot of my hospital bed. I sat cross-legged in a blue dressing gown, still wondering how I had managed to get here. *I feel fine.*

"We found lesions on your brain in the MRI."

"How many?" I dared to ask, not really wanting to know the answer.

"Too many to count," he blithely stated.

"But I feel fine."

"These lesions are very indicative of MS. What do you know about MS?"

My heart fluttered and my breath caught in my throat. "I know it's horrible," I whispered. *This can't be happening. I feel fine. It's just my vision. MS is only a motor disease, right? My retina is detaching or something. That's all. I feel fine!*

In the background, the social worker scribbled in her notebook. That night while waiting for the spinal cord MRI, I would take the opportunity to peek at my folder and her notes. "Patient seemed anxious and upset when told she has MS. When asked what she knew about the disease she said she knew it was an awful disease to have." *I seemed upset, did I? How would you feel, Mrs. Social Worker?* The doctor's report would also state, "Walks with an unsteady gait on the left side." No mention was ever made that a car had run into my left knee the year before. Hence, the stiff gait. No…everything must be MS now.

The neurologist glanced up from his notes and said, "The symptoms of MS can be quite varied. Often optic neuritis, blurry vision, is a first symptom. But symptoms can range from numbness or tingling, balance problems, mental function, incontinence, to nausea and more. Have you noticed anything else?" Seven unmoving faces all stared, waiting for my reply.

I wish I was just going blind.

"No, I'm fine," I said, desperately wanting those words to be true.

"You've never stumbled or tripped without any reason?

I guess your mental function is fine...I see you're a student at Harvard. Does your foot ever fall asleep, or your hand?"

Doesn't everyone's sometime?

I just shook my head. But then I remembered that two months earlier, right after my dad died, when I bent my neck, tingles shot down my legs. *But that was just a pinched nerve, wasn't it?* It had gone away in three weeks, so...no problem. And then there were those annoying foot cramps and spasms, but those had also decreased in frequency from once every day to once every month. *I just didn't have enough magnesium and vitamin D, that's all.*

But I knew at that moment it was true. I had MS. The two things I loved most in life were dance and hiking. I had competed in Irish dance for 12 years and had just gotten my certification to teach competitively. Was that no longer an option? And mountains...I loved the mountains. Born in the Rockies, they were in my blood. I always imagined myself hiking until the day I died. Now the future was uncertain. *What if I can't hike in the future? Would I even be able to walk for much longer?*

Every feeling, twitch, or tingle I ever had or would have over the coming year was scrutinized down to the minutest detail through the MS lens. Fear became the constant battle. For *fear* would infiltrate every aspect of my life. Fear of the unknown. Fear of my future. Fear my husband wouldn't stand by me through this. Fear of not being able to finish my degree. Fear of not being able to pursue the career I wanted. Fear of not being able to pursue my passions of dance and hiking. But most of all, fear of cognitive decline. I'd already watched my father die slowly of dementia, taken from me inch by inch. It was scary enough to think that I could go through that in fifty years. Now it might only be five. Or never. For that is the unpredictability of MS.

October, 2010 – Cambridge, MA

Five months had passed since I was labeled with "MS." One-hundred-twenty days of the same pattern: fear, despair, hope, and determination. Repeat. First fear, followed quickly by despair, and then a glimmer of hope, followed by determination to overcome MS. The cycle could be days, weeks, or hours. Fear, despair, hope....

Every day, the first thought on my mind was, *I have MS*. Every night before I went to bed, I feared waking up with a new symptom. The days when I had no symptoms, no buzzing in my feet, no cramping in my toes, on those days, I felt elation. Hope was easy then. I felt like a normal, young, healthy 27-year-old. Just as I was "supposed" to feel. The days when my feet buzzed every ten minutes were much harder. I sat at work, staring at my computer screen, unmoving. A slight tingle and instantly 100 percent of my focus was on that part of my body. *How large an area is affected?* How long did the sensation last this time? I even used my watch to measure the length of time between tingles. The buzzing didn't hurt, it didn't affect my ability to walk, but it remained a constant reminder. My immune system was attacking my brain and spine. My body was at war, and I was losing.

My mom had clipped out a *Reader's Digest* article about a woman named Lori Schneider, the first person with MS to climb Mt. Everest. She was leading a group of MS patients up Kilimanjaro the following summer, the article said. *Surely the team was already full.*

Kilimanjaro.

I couldn't stop thinking about it. The cycle of fear, despair, and hope continued, but now with a new focus on the hope part. The more I focused on hope, the stronger my determination grew. Determination to conquer the mountain—MS.

I kept thinking, until one day I started an email: *Dear Lori….*

July 18th, 2011 –
Summit day on Mt. Kilimanjaro – 5 a.m.

My feet were getting cold. Every few steps, I felt a hint of cramp.

No! I shouted silently to my body. *You will not cramp. You will be fine. We are almost there.*

But everyone was tired. Even our Tanzanian guide, Auguste, who had probably summited Kilimanjaro a hundred times, started to slow. *Take longer pauses between steps.* I started to worry my feet would cramp from lack of motion in the cold.

Ahead of me, our photographer, Jeff, started to sway.

"Hey Jeff, are you okay?"

He grunted an unintelligible reply.

"Jeff, are you okay?"

"Yeah." He paused for a few seconds. "I am okay."

It didn't take a doctor to see he was not "okay." Finally, I grabbed him by the shoulders. "You have to breathe. I can't hear you breathing." I exaggerated a long breath in and out, audible and forceful, as an example. He started to breathe, and the swaying stopped. His steps grew sure and steady once more.

At Stella's Point, 18,652 feet, our small group of four could smell the summit. We were nearly there. The worst was over. Thankfully, my feet hadn't seized on me to the point I couldn't walk through the spasms. For the first time I knew I would make the summit. *Just another 689 feet.*

We started walking again. False summit after false summit met our steps. Surely it was just around this corner, or just above this ridge. At 19,000 feet, each step is a triumph in and of itself. I was dying of thirst. I couldn't go on without a sip of water. I quickly grabbed the half-frozen Nalgene water bottle out of my pack.

And then I saw the horizon glow with a faint shade of pink. The sun was rising, and the summit lay just a few hundred feet ahead. I felt inexorably drawn ahead. I wanted to run, but the logical side of my brain thought better of it.

Then I saw the summit! Off to my right, huge glaciers were barely visible as the fresh light of dawn peaked over the crater rim.

Tears streamed down my face. *It's so beautiful. I made it!*

Each step grew lighter and lighter, almost like my Irish dance steps. I moved farther and farther ahead from our small group. I wanted to wait, but I couldn't stop. I had so much energy that I wanted to run! To leap at the joy of seeing the summit finally in reach! It was all I could do to not walk any faster than I already was moving, at my usual long-legged gait.

Each step, each breath brought me closer to my goal. For me, climbing Kilimanjaro was triumph in the face of adversity.

Soon I reached the summit. Looking out over the crater, at the dawn sun rising, I lifted my arms to the heavens, lay back my head, and let out a cry of triumph and joy.

I sat on the crater rim for a long time. Our small group, "The A Team," named for our speed, was long gone except for Jeff, our photographer, who valiantly stayed on in the high altitude for many more hours to get everyone's summit shot. Gazing out at the crater, I pulled a small container filled with ashes from my pack. I ached for my dad to be here and tell me it would be okay. More than anything I wanted to tell him that I had MS—to share the pain I had experienced over the past year facing an uncertain future. I prayed to God to send my dad down to look over me, sitting there on the crater rim. I spoke out loud at that moment, saying everything I wanted to tell my dad, trusting that his spirit was with me.

Just as the sun rose, I flung his ashes into the wind over the world's tallest freestanding mountain.

Sarah Conrad is a PhD student at Harvard. In addition to her studies, she loves to write, paint, dance, and now, climb mountains. After being diagnosed with MS at age 26, she immediately felt an overwhelming sense of fear and uncertainty about her future. Meeting Lori and other MS and PD climbers on Kili inspired Sarah to live a more awesome life with MS than she would have lived without it. In that spirit she recently launched a website: www. LiveAwesomewithMS.com where her blog covers MS-

related research and provides inspiring ideas of how to lead your best life in spite of MS.

Breathe

Stephanie Ludlow

IN APRIL OF 2006, AFTER I GRADUATED FROM Northern Michigan University, my body began to go numb. Unable to keep my body temperature regulated, I felt numbness on my skin from head to toe. My eyes did not focus properly, consistently blurring, twitching almost, so that the simple act of focusing on a step became difficult.

Because I did not have health insurance, I sought help from a walk-in clinic in an attempt to find out what was happening. After multiple visits, their diagnosis was anxiety, insomnia, and restless arm syndrome, but none of it fully made sense to me. A month later the symptoms went away, but I was not completely back to normal. I still had spells of numbness and muscle spasms. I continued on with life not knowing what was going on with my body, not knowing that my body was attacking itself.

That spring, I moved to the Pacific Northwest for an AmeriCorps job. Three years later, in October 2008, I decided to make a switch to continue my education and go to physical therapy school. In December of that year, I left my job and began teaching Pilates. I had a sore shoulder at the time, so I went to the doctor to have it checked before my AmeriCorps insurance ran out at the end of the year. I told the doctor that I believed a muscle was pinching a nerve, because from the hips down, I was numb. I explained that my symptoms from previous years had never fully gone away, so she requested an MRI. They called me that same day to come in for a second scan to verify their suspicions. Later that week I heard the words, "You have MS."

It was New Year's Eve. I had a port in my arm for a three-day regimen of steroid infusions. I was numb from the symptoms, diagnosis, and treatment. And I was scared. I could not fathom the idea that I had this disease and sought the opinions of two other neurologists. By March 2009, through a series of diagnostic tests, I had three neurologists confirm the diagnosis. What I learned is that multiple sclerosis is a chronic demyelinating disease of the central nervous system. With MS, the body's immune defense system attacks the myelin sheath of nerves in the central nervous system, producing a variety of symptoms ranging from cognitive impairments to the inability to walk.

I never once asked, "Why me?" or exclaimed, "My life is over." I did not want to waste my time in that black hole. Instead, I immediately immersed myself in the MS community for support. No longer having insurance, I tried every natural alternative therapy, but in December I had a relapse and by February 2010, I was on injection-based, disease-modifying medication. I adopted the motto to live life 60 minutes at a time and not think about what I might lose later in life—to appreciate what I have at the present moment.

Later that year, while picking up a couch from my friend Sean's house, he told me, "I'm going to Africa. You should think about it too, Steph. No really, check out this woman, Lori Schneider. She is amazing." My immediate thoughts were: *No way, not possible. I'll never have enough money to afford a trip like that. I'll never be able to get time off work, not to mention, that my MS will never let me endure such a taxing overseas adventure.*

Then, my inner self slapped me in the face, reminding me that anything is possible. And so the journey began—training, fundraising, and most importantly, the relationships that emerged between fellow climbers, my community, friends, and of course, Sean.

At times, I doubted my abilities to see this through, because I continued to experience numbness, fatigue, and restless nights from sore and spastic muscles. The list went on as I prepared for this adventure of a lifetime. I tested my MS, taxed my energies, and found that yoga and swimming balanced the arduous training and my doubting mind. The best thing I could do for myself was enjoy the life I'd been given and appreciate my abilities.

Finally, the day came for Sean and me to board the plane to meet what are now lifelong friends and ascend the world's tallest freestanding mountain. Exhausted from travel, introductions, gear checks, safety instructions, and the reality that this was really happening, our team of 31 loaded into 2 small vans and arrived at the trailhead.

Backpacks loaded, porters already miles ahead of us, smiles all around, we hiked up the pathway that would lead to the ultimate zenith.

I remember vividly our first lunch stop. On the side of the trail was a table and chairs set up colonial style. Plastic pink flowers in a vase on the tablecloth greeted us, along with cups, plates, utensils, and a plethora of powdered drinks and teas. This was my first exposure to powdered protein-enriched milk drinks like Milo, a real lifesaver for the long strenuous days we endured. We washed our hands with warm water. That's right, warm water. Our porters served us lunch and as soon as we were done, the hiking continued.

As our guides instructed, I breathed deeply and efficiently to calm my headache and cope with the low levels of oxygen in the air. Six days of hiking high, five nights of sleeping low, we gradually climbed our way up to High Camp, our summit staging place. With just a few hours of sleep, our guides woke us at 10:00 p.m. on July 17th to begin our long trek to the top of Uhuru.

With deep breaths of high altitude air and walking "pole-pole," one foot in front of the other, our pace took us slowly through the darkness. Elated from the epic hiking days we'd had thus far, the first half of the summit passed by. One lucid memory I hold is the song of the porters' voices chanting the rhythm of our pace. The line of headlamps illuminated the path above and below, showing the number of brave souls awakening the slopes of the mountain. Our immediate goal was to make it to Stella Point, which would end the steep grade and give a sense of relief to our tired, aching calves. Gasping for air, tears streaming down our cold cheeks, Sean and I hugged and laughed. We cried together as we rejoiced on Stella Point with our fellow teammates. We had made it, wow! We made it!

At that point we followed the trail as it gradually ascended around the crater rim to the summit. Although it was just a few more hours, they were definitely the toughest hours on the mountain. Despite MS, fatigue, frozen toes and fingers, iced-over Nalgene's, gasping for air, and stumbling, we reached the wooden sign that announced,

CONGRATULATIONS! YOU ARE NOW AT UHURU PEAK, TANZANIA, 5895M AMSL. AFRICA'S HIGHEST POINT. WORLD'S HIGHEST FREESTANDING MOUNTAIN.

The rewarding feeling of accomplishment, the views, and the support around me were indescribable. The fortune of this moment was greater than all the riches in the world. I took a deep breath, absorbed it all in, stored it deep within my lungs, my heart, and my soul, and thought, I am alive!

The reason I did the climb was simple. I will not be restricted in my life by this debilitating condition. However, this journey gave me so much more than simply defying MS. I met the most amazing group of lifelong companions, supporters, and fellow adventurers. I learned the importance of appreciating myself, being confident, being present, and most of all, breathing. My motto now includes the importance of deep, meaningful, purposeful breath. Today I remind myself, "60 minutes at a time just breathe."

Thank you, Uhuru, for showing me the practice of breathing consciously. I use it every day to get through the struggle, to bring clarity into a moment. Thank you, Sean, for lighting the fire inside me that still burns today. Thank you to my companion climber, Paula, for your support and love. You have a heart of gold. And most importantly— thank you, Lori, for bringing us all together. Day by day, 60 minutes at a time, with deep, focused breaths, I continue to overcome the burdens of this illness and stay on track to achieve my dreams. Thank you everyone for being a part of this life adventure!

*Born in Michigan, **Stephanie Ludlow** now lives in Hood River, Oregon, where she is an outdoor enthusiast, swimmer and avid yogi. She loves to cook and enjoys wine and microbrews. An amazing group of friends, a supportive family and the sweet dog, Hannah Bear are by her side. Her strong belief in physical and food-based healing constitutes her treatment for MS. She is an advocate for community health and is actively involved in her surrounding community. Currently, she is chasing her dream to become a prominent physical therapist, working towards the incorporation of motion therapy into treatment for neurological conditions. After graduation she plans to volunteer abroad and share her knowledge and passion for physical health and well-being.*

Beyond Our Limits

"The only way to discover the limits of the possible is to go beyond them into the impossible."
- Arthur C. Clarke

That's What Friends Are For

Jeanne Van Hulle

POLE, POLE IS AN APT MANTRA FOR MOUNTAIN climbing and for life in general. I learned this term in Tanzania the summer I joined a very special group of people to climb Mt. Kilimanjaro. *Slowly, slowly* in Swahili is the relaxed way to get to wherever it is you are going. In fact, life in Africa is much slower paced than stateside. A trip like this is indeed a healthy way to step out of everyday life and into a whole new world, immersing you slowly into an altered reality where time crawls and focus sharpens.

This new world was like being in Lion King Boot Camp. My role in this expedition was as a companion climber to a young woman with MS. We had a shared goal to face life's challenges without fear or give into a diagnosis. There are no lives without challenges, and this trip tapped into the power of shared hope.

I generally live a very settled life in Davenport, Iowa as a 56-year-old second grade teacher and mother of two grown sons. I have never lived outside the state of Iowa, and I am rather proud of that dubious honor. I am deeply rooted in the cornfields and river bluffs along the

Mississippi River of my hometown. I liken my life to being in a box, but a rather nice box of my own design.

Enter my dear friend, Lori Schneider, mountaineer and decimator of boxes! Her life is as out of the box as you can get, scaling the highest peaks in the world all the while inspiring others with her words and actions. Lori lives with a diagnosis of multiple sclerosis and has made it her life's work to help others with such a diagnosis, empowering them to achieve great things through adventure.

This special friendship began back in 1974 when Lori and I met our first night of college at Clarke College in Dubuque, Iowa. Clarke was an all-girls Catholic college, and we bonded over our shared major in education, flirting with boys and holding late night study sessions. This friendship has endured what I think of as the three D's: divorce, death, and disease. We have celebrated and commiserated for over 30 years. So, when Lori invited me on this adventure what could I say but yes?

The yes I gave Lori seemed regrettable and insane that cold night in July while we were on our final summit attempt of Mt. Kilimanjaro. *What in the world was a woman from Iowa doing so far outside her safe and warm box?* It was after midnight when I plopped down on a large boulder on the mountainside, fighting the nausea that had overwhelmed me at High Camp as we prepared for summiting. My climbing partner, April, was in extreme pain from her MS as we inched our way, *pole, pole* up the scree-covered slope. We so wanted to make it to the top and were reaching deep into our souls for strength and stamina. We tried to keep eating and drinking for energy but were finding it hard to continue climbing in the face of our exhaustion and altitude sickness.

One of my favorite, albeit poignant, moments of the trip occurred when we both sat down on a rock and knew our personal summits had been met at 16,100 feet. We didn't really have to debate; we both just knew it was time. Without a spoken word between us, we understood that we had given it our all, but the time had come to stop trying to climb higher. My altitude sickness symptoms had become unbearable as had April's pain levels. One guide assisted the two of us in our descent. He understood how imperative it was for both of us to get to a lower elevation as quickly as possible. No more *pole, pole*. No more pushing upward. There is a time for being slow and a time where the need for speed overrides all else—we both needed expeditious action.

April and I rested, grateful to be safe and warm in our tent as the others kept going. We heard people returning, some having made it and others like us turning back with various altitude-related ailments. I felt a mixture of sadness, joy, and utter exhaustion. After having trained extensively for so many months, I had truly wanted to reach that summit. Yet, I understood that for my personal safety, it became necessary to descend and return to camp. There are defining moments in life where we face myriad emotions and gain clarity of vision. This was such a moment for me—I felt very alive and focused in my exhaustion. Yet, even with this clear perspective, if I could have been teleported back to my safe Iowa home I would have. *Please, give me back my box.* I wanted to crawl inside, tape up the openings, and shut out the world. I guess exhaustion, altitude sickness, and nausea do not a happy camper make.

An important part of our trip had been the joining of a healthy climber partnered with a climber with MS or Parkinson's. Living just across the river from each other, my partner, April, and I were able to take hikes and train together. We even got to know each other's families prior to the trip. She was a brave climber in the face of some very tough symptoms from her MS. The pain she was fighting grew as the climb progressed until she had to be carried off the mountain on the final day. The downward trip on a metal cart was a difficult one—there was nothing relaxing about it. Between the severity of her pain and the jolting and bouncing of the cart that she endured as they made their way back to civilization, her pain increased. She later joked that it might have been easier to have just been left on the mountain!

I found it funny that I was considered the healthy climber, because I had been diagnosed with rheumatoid arthritis in October of 2010, after I had already committed to the climb. This diagnosis served to strengthen my determination to make this trip since I didn't know if it might be my last big physical adventure. I had already been forced to give up running due to back problems that resulted in a surgery. I still miss running every day but don't regret the 30 years of pursuing that sport, including several half marathons and the full Chicago Marathon.

During the months leading up to the climb, as I fought the pain that was especially bad in my legs, I often couldn't sleep for more than a few hours a night. On those long, hurtful nights I questioned so many things in my life, including this crazy trip. Those were the times when I sank into my personal heart of darkness and felt terror and a horrible sense of loss. I had been so proud of being healthy and strong with a cheerful outlook on life, and this was all slipping away from me. I became even more frightened after I learned what can happen to a person with RA. Not only do joints become more inflamed and damaged, but systemic damage can occur to various organs, such as heart and liver. However, my rheumatologist was very encouraging and positive about me making the trip and felt that being and staying active was vitally important to my overall prognosis.

During those months after my diagnosis, as I tried to come to terms with what RA might mean to my life, it was the training and required focus that pulled me through. I kept hiking, lifting weights, going to physical therapy, and getting injections to keep the pain down. My acupuncturist, massage therapist, and trainer at the Y all kept me going, as did my family, friends, and my second grade students. I had hope because I had a goal and a purpose outside of my normal life. My safe little box had been filled with pain and worry, leaving me eager to flee. I was determined to attack this mountain and my new life and live with my diagnosis in dignity. Slowly, slowly, I became stronger and felt back in control.

I brought back some wonderful souvenirs from Africa, though most were not tangible. I discovered that a shared purpose leads to wonderful discoveries of strength and hope in the face of life's sometimes crushing challenges. I still have rheumatoid arthritis, April and the others still have MS and Parkinson's. We also have this incredible experience that has bonded us together for life. We have climbed out of the drabness of daily life and into an atmosphere filled with joy and incredible beauty. We have climbed above the clouds for a stellar view of a connected world of people sharing both triumphs and tragedies. The grace, kindness, and beauty of the people of Tanzania will stay with all of us. Our entire group of climbers, guides, porters, and cooks were inspirational and will continue to enrich my life.

I am safely back in my box, and on the whole, glad to be here. I have left the lid off, however, so that I can spot new opportunities and adventures when they beckon. The memories keep me warm and continually amaze me when I look at a picture or get an email from a fellow climber. Did I really do that? What will I do next? Just yesterday, I got a brochure about a walking tour of Tuscany, and there's always Machu Picchu, or Colorado, and so on, and so on. Once you've been empowered through adventure, it is indeed more than a mountain that you experience and conquer.

Jeanne Van Hulle is a lifelong resident of the very flat state of Iowa, so climbing anything; much less Mt. Kilimanjaro, was indeed quite a leap of faith. In 1974, she met this trip's inspired leader, Lori Schneider, during the first night of college at Clarke College in Dubuque, Iowa. They have remained close friends and fellow adventure seekers ever since. Jeanne's teaching career has focused on showing all children, especially those with special needs, that learning can be wonderful, exciting and worthwhile. She is incredibly proud of her two sons, Patrick and Michael, who are living adventure-filled lives of their own. She can't wait to see what new experiences await her and knows that the lessons learned on an African mountain and the strengths of her fellow climbers will help sustain her through whatever life brings. jvanhulle6547@msn.com.

Reflections of
a Summit

Ines Grau

FINALLY IN OXYGENATED LAND. AFTER HAVING A nice dinner to celebrate our summit, I can't stop thinking about everything that happened during the past six days. It all looks like a dream now.

It seems as if it were yesterday when I was departing to Africa, afraid and nervous about meeting the team and getting to know each person I had the pleasure to ultimately climb alongside. *This amazing team!*

I could tell you that ten of us had MS and four others had Parkinson's disease, but now, after living what I have lived, it makes no sense at all trying to distinguish ourselves in this way. We have clearly shown that our diseases do not define us—nor do they have to keep us separate. We were all part of an amazing group of people—of spirited adventurers—who climbed Kilimanjaro together.

Seven people out of the twenty-nine were not able to make it to the top of the mountain, but without any ounce of doubt, they did accomplish their personal Summit. We all gave everything we had to give, beginning with the unimaginable and ending with what we thought was non-existing in us.

We left the basecamp at 10:30 p.m. on Sunday and we summited about 9:00 a.m. Monday morning. I think that was the longest night I've ever experienced in my entire life. The route seemed unachievable and the lack of oxygen and absence of sunlight pushed us all enough to consider sending this most significant part of our adventure to hell in order to return to our sweet homes. But this adventure meant something significant, and there was a consistent reason for fighting, suffering, and continuing onward. We had the opportunity to scream to the world that even though we were diagnosed with a disease, we could do it, and that became our engine for forward movement.

After frozen food and drinks and bouts of nausea because of the lack of oxygen, I fed myself glucose pills that slowly gave my muscles the energy I needed to reach the roof of Africa. With a steady rhythm of right leg BREATHE, left leg BREATHE, I continued that way for ten long hours. When we reached 5,200 meters, the first symptoms appeared indicating that I needed oxygen—headache and nausea. So I took an ibuprofen and continued to breathe and climb.

And then it happened. I summited! Once there, I could only shout: UAAAAAHAHAUJA!!

I had imagined for a whole year what I would do once I reached the summit, but when the moment arrived, I could only take some pictures and then head back down. My headache was increasing and people's voices began to mix with my thoughts, as if I were in a deep dream.

I didn't know at that moment, but I had achieved a dream I first believed would be unachievable. Now, I am left feeling immense admiration for the rest of the team—all of them so strong, so full of life.

Hopefully, there is no way back for any of us. I do not know if I will ever climb Kilimanjaro again, but without a doubt I will continue to face the different obstacles and opportunities that life presents for me, just placing one step in front of the other and always, always "above our limits," as my dear Lori says.

Out of this adventure—this accomplishment—we have opened a new path in our lives. A bigger adventure full of emotions has begun. We have achieved the opening of our own way. And I believe, from this experience, we have two things to remember day after day:

Do not lose the path we have been following!

and

Do not believe that our fears tire our bodies!

Just like this, we will achieve the

summits that are yet to come.

Ines Grau *is a 25-year-old woman from Spain, who has a huge number of goals for her life. She is a psychologist and feels that life is not about living. Rather, it is about feeling alive. She believes that every person in this world has something to give, and she tries to give the world the best of herself. She does not believe in defeats, in "I can'ts," nor in yesterdays. She is not afraid of looking for that something that makes her feel stronger, even if that something is hidden on the highest peak of Africa. You can follow Ines' blog at http://mueveteporlaem.wordpress.com*

I May Never Have this Chance in My Life Again

April Winckler

MY NAME IS APRIL WINCKLER. BEFORE MS, I WAS a varsity tennis player. I rollerbladed everywhere. I rode my bike. My life was active and very full. I worked and attended school full-time. I was always on the go.

The first symptom I had at 16 years old was optic neuritis. Then one day, I became unable to walk straight. My right side was weak, and I appeared drunk. I went to the hospital where they performed neurological tests. I had an MRI and a spinal tap. Then, I got my answer—I was told I had MS.

After my diagnosis, I felt a little scared. I didn't really know what MS was. Once I learned more about multiple sclerosis, I began to deal with what I would be facing.

I was invited to go on the climb after I heard Lori Schneider give the keynote address at a fundraiser for Davenport Community Schools, where one of the other climbers, Jeanne Van Hulle, works. I and my husband attended, and I was very impressed and filled with hope after hearing Lori speak.

At first I didn't think I would do it. Then I thought I

might never have this chance in my life again. So I decided to go on the climb, and I worked very hard to train. Jeanne became my training partner as I prepared for the opportunity of a lifetime. I walked up and down hills with my backpack on. It was very tiring but I was determined.

On the mountain I felt amazing. I felt like MS wasn't going to keep me down. I have secondary progressive MS and had taken 20 shots in my legs to help manage the extreme MS-related pain in order to climb the mountain. On the last day, I made it up to 16,500 feet. For me, this was the greatest accomplishment I'd ever achieved. Along with experiencing my first plane ride and first time ever outside the United States to get to Mt. Kilimanjaro, I had climbed to a height most of us only dream of doing.

On the last day, fatigue and pain took over in my legs and I had to be carried off the mountain. But, I took with me all that I had shared with others on our team and my own achievements. I will carry this with me for the rest of my life.

I thank Lori for the opportunity to be a part of this great experience.

April Winckler *has lived an athletic lifestyle in the past, with a passion for tennis, swimming, and rollerblading. She also enjoys watching movies along with her devoted husband Patrick. April lives with progressive MS and sometimes uses a walker or wheelchair for assistance. April trained for the Kilimanjaro climb by walking daily to keep her body and muscles strong. April often has pain associated with her MS and works closely with her doctors to monitor and control her symptoms. April hopes to someday learn to scuba dive.*

Our Fountain of Youth

"There is a fountain of youth. It is your
mind, your talents, the creativity you bring to
your life and the lives of the people you love.
When you learn to tap this source, you will
truly have defeated age."
- Sophia Loren

Shall We Climb?

Connie Kemmerer

FOR ME, THE KILIMANJARO CLIMB WAS A REENTRY into life. A year earlier I had been in a wheelchair and walking with a walker. I do not have MS or Parkinson's, though my mother had something similar to Parkinson's. I had back failure, mostly due to having an active and adventurous life.

In 2003, I founded Teton Wellness Institute. We invited Lori Schneider to come and speak in 2010 about her amazing Seven Summit climbs that she'd made after being diagnosed with MS. Hearing her story, I knew I wanted to join her Kilimanjaro group as a companion climber, but with my own injuries I wasn't sure I could do it.

After two surgeries and a lot of rehab, I felt I could be a supportive companion. Concentrating on someone else making it to the summit would be good therapy for me too. I had been a mountaineer and ascent climber before so I knew what it would take. In fact, I had climbed Kilimanjaro 45 years earlier. And I wanted to see it again. Five weeks before the departure date, I called Lori and asked if by chance she needed a support climber. She did. I would go.

My fellow climber, Kristy Banaszak, was a small, spirited young woman who had been dealing with MS for five years. Seven inches shorter than I am, she was filled with such energy that she reminded me of *the little engine that could*. Kristy engaged everyone with her enthusiasm and humor. She continues to inspire me to this day, especially in the charismatic way she built a team of support and friendship around her. I was later able to use her example when I continued on to climb Mt. Kenya by myself with a small team comprised of a porter, cook, and guide.

On the summit day, Kristy, our guide Mathew, and I climbed with determination. We continued our ascent with such focus that we weren't able to see when Kristy began to have trouble. Besides MS, she has asthma that kicked in at 18,700 feet. For Kristy it was time to go down.

I had wondered what I would do if I had to choose between Kristy and the summit. I'd even discussed it with our Alpine Ascent group leader, Eric. It turned out there was no need for debate. I would stay with my friend. However, on the descent I passed Eric who told me to turn around and go for the summit. "Kristy has oxygen, Mathew, and another guide to support her. She will be fine," he assured me. He pointed out, though, that there were no more guides for me. "Just climb until you find others of our group," he instructed.

Step, breath, step breath. Calm, mesmerizing. The heartbeat of movement.

On the final ascent, I was fortunate to meet up with Ines and Lori. What a gift to walk with another and just breathe—a chance to be me, yet a part of something so much grander—life, friendships, the earth. I was filled with joy and gratitude.

So *this* is why I came—in helping another, I experienced the unexpected rediscovery of my own determination and will to live life fully. I reconnected with the essence of my personal power and the rhythm of life. No, I'm not too old or crippled. Just as MS and Parkinson's are not an end to life, my life is not over.

The summit was spectacular. Less snow than 45 years ago. More people on the route, but also more friends. And…more life.

Connie Kemmerer PhD, LMT is the owner of the Jackson Hole Mountain Resort, along with her brother and sister. She is also founder and chair of Teton Wellness Institute. Connie moved from Sun Valley, Idaho, to Jackson Hole 20 years ago to participate as an owner of the resort and has contributed to creating a world class year-round resort. Ten years ago, along with a group of doctors and practitioners, Connie founded the Integrative Healthcare Foundation, now known as The Teton Wellness Institute. This organization, which began with a wellness festival and programs to educate and empower personal health, led to a community resource center, a Chamber of Commerce program called Destination Wellness, employee and corporate wellness programs, and the creation of a health and wellness department in the local hospital. Connie's interest in health and spirituality go back to her teenage years when she worked with missionaries in Africa. She later earned her PhD in anthropology, became a childbirth educator, massage therapist, started a church (Light on Mountains Spiritual Center, Sun Valley, Idaho) and worked with Discovery, a personal growth program operating in Idaho and New Zealand. Connie's greatest dream is to experience life fully while making a difference and a contribution to the world. "Global peace, health and sustainability begin within."

My Daughter, My Friend

Neal Schneider

AS A FATHER OF FOUR, RAISING CHILDREN BACK in the 50's, our family life was very much a traditional one. I went to work each day while our children were brought up by their stay-at-home mom, my beautiful wife, Dee. My job was to make money and have a career; hers was to care for the family and create a loving home for all of us. When decisions needed to be made, most often I told my three sons and one daughter, "Ask your mother." She was in charge of making sure things ran smoothly, and she took great pride in raising a family of strong, often independent children.

As a way to deal with the stresses of life, I created a daily routine of going for an early-morning run to clear my head before the hectic day started. Four-thirty was my usual wakeup call, with a run of several miles, often a quick stop at church as I passed by, then home to start my workday. Dee fed the kids, ironed my suit, and sent us all on our way. Life continued like that for most of our 48 years of marriage.

In 1974, my only daughter, Lori, began running with

me from time to time. I think it was more about her desire for us to spend time together than an actual love of the sport, but it was a time for us to bond as friends instead of interacting in the typical parent-child relationship.

One day, I attended a lunch meeting and the speaker talked about his recent experiences climbing Kilimanjaro. I was 40 years old, with a full-time career and a full-time family. Climbing mountains was not something I had ever done or ever thought about doing. That evening I was in the kitchen and mentioned to Lori that someday I would like to go to Africa and climb Mt. Kilimanjaro. She told me that some day she would go with me, and the seeds for our shared dream were planted.

Time went on, 20 years went by, and the kids grew up and moved away to start their own lives and families. I was still getting up at 4:30 a.m. for my morning exercise, although my runs had changed to walks in respect of my 60-year-old knees. Lori had moved to Colorado and had been teaching children for 15 years. She and her husband had decided to take a leave of absence from their jobs to pursue a dream of traveling the world. Lori had always possessed a sense of adventure and a love of travel, so after saving money for nearly ten years, they planned to leave for a two-year adventure.

Plans were made to spend a few months in Africa during their travels. *Africa, Kilimanjaro, climbing, climbing together as a father-daughter team*…all thoughts that crept in, reminding me that *just maybe* this idea from so many years ago *might actually* become a reality. Ideas were discussed, arrangements were made, and before we knew it, we were meeting in Africa, one year after Lori and her husband had left the United States on their journey.

Although we had both trained for the climb for nearly a year in advance, mountain climbing is difficult, exhausting, and always unpredictable. You cannot plan for things like illness, energy levels, altitude sickness, or injury. We set off with high hopes, big dreams, and a level of excitement that propelled us forward with every step. As the steps got more and more difficult and the air got thinner and thinner, our energy was further zapped by each gain in elevation that we achieved. As we hiked, Lori forced me to eat and drink, even though I had no appetite.

We laughed as we went through father-daughter firsts, like sharing a tiny tent or cabin together or peeing behind a rock to retain the smallest amount of privacy. The daughter my wife and I had raised to use her voice and be independent now took over the role of "boss" when it came to reminding me of all I needed to do to stay healthy on the mountain. I listened when she told me to take care of my feet, to change out of the sweat-soaked t-shirt I was wearing, to eat another cardboard-tasting energy bar, and to put on more sunscreen. When had our roles in life reversed?

Summit night came and we were ready to put all of our training to the test. Up at 1:00 a.m., multiple layers of warm clothes on our bodies, headlamps and spare batteries in place, food and water in our pockets, and packs on our backs. We were ready! We began the trudge toward the 19,340-foot summit with both nervousness and excitement. If we were to make it to the very top, we would be summiting on my 61st birthday, June 7, 1993.

The pace was slow as we scrambled over large boulders

and navigated dusty, scree-filled slopes in the dark and cold. As we neared Gilman's Point, we hoped we were at the summit, but our guide said we had another hour to go. Lori forced me to drink water and take a bite of food, but I was feeling the effects of the altitude and the nausea that came with it.

The rocks had changed to snow, and with each step we sunk deep on the untracked route our guide had chosen. Our pace slowed to a crawl, but we could see the summit ahead. Only 100 feet to go and we would reach Uhuru Peak, the highest point in Africa. I turned to Lori and said I didn't think I could make it. She looked at me and said she didn't think she could make it either. At that moment, we hooked arm-in-arm, and I think we dragged each other those final steps to the summit. We had made it, but what I remember was the real need to sit down and catch my breath on the snow hump in front of the summit sign. We shook our heads in amazement when our young guide took out a cigarette, had trouble lighting the match, and then smoked it as we took our labored breaths and photos.

Lori had brought along a small birthday cake in her pack, but it was frozen solid. I tried to gnaw off a small bite to please her, but I was feeling so sick that I couldn't. She also placed a medal around my neck and told me how much she loved me. With only a few minutes on top, it was time to make the long journey back down and tell Dee and our sons, Bill, Joe, and Dan, that we were both alive and safe.

Fast forward to 1999. You know how you can have

selective amnesia after having done something so difficult that you wonder how you ever managed to succeed, but as time goes by, you remember it as not so bad? Well, I think that is what happened to us after a six-year gap between climbing adventures. Lori and I decided that it might be fun to do another climb together, and somehow the wheels were set in motion for a climb of Mt. Aconcagua, the highest peak in South America. If we made it this time, we would stand on the summit on the millennium, New Year's Eve 1999-2000.

At 67, I was still walking daily, but now I was doing my early-morning walks with a pack on my back. Lori, who was living in Colorado, was training hard on her end as well. Then, life took a terrible twist. Lori woke up one day with unexplained numbness and tingling in her body. She was training hard, and Dee and I thought the numbness might be the result of a cortisone shot she had recently received in her foot. She continued to go through tests to determine the cause of the numbness but was pretty quiet about it all. She continued to train as best she could, because this trip was extremely important to her. She later told me that she had been afraid I would say we couldn't go on the climb if I had known the real reason for her numbness.

Lori was diagnosed with multiple sclerosis, a disease that sounded horrible and one that none of us really knew anything about. Shock turned to disbelief, disbelief turned to sadness, and sadness turned to a feeling of helplessness as our family feared along with her. Days and months went by, and I think Lori needed to prove to herself that she was still strong in spite of what the disease MS did to her emotionally and physically. She was determined to attempt the climb and move beyond the fear she was feeling. You see, Lori had been hiding the illness from everyone but her family and two best friends, and this secret was eating away at her spirit.

We were at 18,500 feet, high on Mt. Aconcagua. The going was slow at that elevation, and I was feeling plagued by that old friend, altitude sickness, which had visited me on Kilimanjaro just six years earlier. Lori tried to get me to eat and drink that day, but I was feeling sick and couldn't. This mountain took so much more energy than Kilimanjaro because we did most sections of the climb twice.

We had to carry a load to a higher camp, drop our gear, then go back down and rest for the night. The next day, we brought the tents and the remainder of our gear back up to the point we had reached the day before. This approach is about acclimatizing by climbing high and sleeping low and it is used on mountains like Aconcagua where the summit is nearly 23,000 feet high. The constant up and down took a toll on my energy, as did the elevation that seemed to steal every breath from my lungs. I was nauseous and knew that I had to turn around. Altitude sickness is deadly, as we had learned the previous day when a young woman from a Mexican climbing team died during the night and returned to base camp in a body bag.

I called ahead to Lori; she stopped and turned. I told her that this was my summit and I needed to head back down. She hurried to where I was standing and we hugged with tears in our eyes. I told her that she needed to go on because I knew she could make it. I worried about sending my daughter with MS to the summit, just as she worried about sending me back down with a guide and altitude sickness. Three days later we were reunited as she returned from an empowering summit that changed her life and reminded her of her inner strength.

Many years have gone by and so much has changed in both of our lives. My wife of nearly 50 years died suddenly but peacefully in 2002 from heart disease that we didn't know she had. It was a pain so deep that it is still hard to believe she is really gone. Our family was shaped by her love and dedication as a mom, and she is missed more than words can say.

Lori's life changed too, and after her MS diagnosis, her marriage ended. Her life today represents using all that she has learned about overcoming fear to help others move forward after a diagnosis. I am proud of what she has accomplished in the world of climbing but most of all for how she has helped others move beyond their own fears of MS and begin to live life again.

For me, the 2011 Kilimanjaro Leap of Faith climb was a chance for our climbing story to come full circle. At age 79, it was a chance to climb another mountain with my daughter, my friend. This would be a partnered climb, where each person with MS or Parkinson's disease was paired with a healthy climbing partner to support them every step of the way. As a companion climber, it wasn't about making the summit for yourself, but to help your partner move beyond their own fear and doubt. I was honored when Lori asked me to be her partner. I love her and I know she loves me too. I knew this would be a powerful experience for both of us.

So my preparations for Kilimanjaro 2011 were much the same as they had been back in 1993, except I was now 18 years older. I walked each morning at 4:30 a.m., with a new, lighter pack the kids had given me for Christmas. Of course, Lori insisted that the father of the leader be dressed nicely, so on this trip, all of my clothes were color coordinated with my pack, thanks to more Christmas gifts, which I am sure she picked out. New poles, boots, water bottles—you name it. If I couldn't make the summit, at least I was going to look good trying.

This trip to Kili seemed even tougher than the last—for both of us. Yes, part of it was due to the fact that we were both much older, but the rocky terrain on this more accessible side of the mountain was very new to me. We had our work cut out for us, but we were both feeling up to the challenge. It was a matter of what the mountain would do to me in terms of elevation and altitude issues. Altitude is the great equalizer, where the weak can seem strong and the strong can seem weak, depending on the day. For me, on summit night I was feeling the latter.

We started out with headlamps—snaking our way up the scree-covered slopes—and memories of our earlier Kili climb 18 years ago still fresh. Lori followed me, along with our personal porters, who helped when a step turned to a scramble as we went up and around large rocks and ledges. Hour after hour in the cold and dark, we made the slow march toward the summit.

Every time we stopped to rest, my daughter told me to eat one of those awful gel packets that seemed impossible to slide down my throat. Many times she opened them for me and held them to my lips, determined to keep my energy strong. I balked at the thought, not sure I could even hold it down long enough to do any good. She opened my water and handed it to me, even with my protests of not being thirsty. She was a seasoned climber by this point in the game and was concerned for my safety. Ultimately, she looked at me and told me that if I had any hope of making it safely, I had to eat when I wasn't hungry and drink when I wasn't thirsty. I finally succumbed to the pressure and said, "OK boss." We both laughed and I decided it was better not to fight her judgment on this one. I said those two words many times that night.

Dawn was breaking and it energized us to see the light of day beginning to hide the shadows of the night. In the light, we could see the rim of the crater up ahead. To me, it looked close enough to touch, but our guide said it would take at least another hour to make the rim, then an hour or more to the summit from there, given our pace and rest breaks. I was exhausted and needed to sit down.

I looked at Lori and asked her what she thought. She had such love and concern in her eyes as she told me she loved me more than the mountain. She reminded me I had already summited once and thought it might not be worth it to push so hard a second time. She said she knew I could make it, but wondered if I would have the strength to make the long climb back down. I said those words one more time, "OK boss," as we hugged each other. My legs felt weak and I was thankful for the two strong, surefooted African guides who led me down the steep, rocky slopes that early morning. Their knowledge of the mountain was a lifeline to all of us who pushed our boundaries on a climb like Kili.

Back at High Camp, I sat with my sore, tired feet in a bowl of warm water that the porters had prepared. I watched as each exhausted climber came down and quickly found a spot to rest. Words were few, but we had shared an experience beyond words. Each of us—whether we made the summit or not—had reached our own personal summit. As a companion climber, we had helped someone else realize *their* dream, *their* goal, and by doing so, we had all reached ours as well.

To the climbers with MS and PD, your strength and courage are a positive example for all of us about moving past fear and not being afraid to try. I'd climb with you again any day.

By the way, my next mountain will be Space Mountain in Disney World.

*Our eldest member of the Leap of Faith team, **Neal Schneider**, proved it's never too late to dream big. Scaling vertical rock walls, trudging for hours over rugged terrain and sleeping on frigid ground were not things Neal normally aspired to achieve. That is, not until he decided to leave the comfort of his Janesville, Wisconsin home and family funeral business for yet another adventure with his daughter, Lori. Neal, a Korean War veteran, was no stranger to hard work. He and his wife Dee lived a typical small town lifestyle, raising their four children—Bill, Lori, Joe, and Dan. Neal taught his children to be honest and compassionate, to give back to the community and to never be afraid to take risks. At 80, he still lives by those rules and reminds us all* *that we are never too old to try. Five generations of caring and compassion: www.schneiderfuneraldirectors.com.*

The Spirit Moves Us

"In the silence of the heart, God speaks."
- Mother Teresa

Finding My Way

Martha Carlin

JULY 18, 2011, ON THE SUMMIT OF MOUNT Kilimanjaro I opened my heart fully for the very first time and was overwhelmed by love.

My husband, John, has Parkinson's disease. Along with others diagnosed with PD and multiple sclerosis, he was invited by the Leap of Faith group to climb Mount Kilimanjaro. He asked me if I wanted to be his healthy climbing companion. Climbing a mountain had never been on my bucket list, but I thought *Why not?*

I started training in October for the July climb because I wasn't in the same kind of shape as John. To reduce his symptoms from PD, he had kept to a rigorous biking program four days a week since 2007. I, on the other hand, had not exercised regularly since graduating from college.

About six weeks before we were to leave, we started training together, taking long hikes in the Colorado mountains. These treks allowed us many private hours, which we hadn't shared together since before our children were born over a decade earlier. I treasured this time for just the two of us. It renewed and refreshed our relationship as we talked about our lives and dreams of future adventures.

In the last weeks leading up to the climb, we increased our training and spent hours checking and rechecking our gear. With John's direction, our basement floor had been sectioned off as a staging area—clothing, socks, sleeping bag and pad, water bottles, water treatments, first aid/blister protection, energy bars, coats, gloves, packs, head lamps, Diamox for altitude sickness, Cipro for infection. John is an experienced camper, Eagle Scout, and my personal Sherpa for every adventure—he is always prepared. Being more of a fly-by-the-seat-of-my-pants kind of gal, I valued his expertise and organizational skills—he thought of everything!

I was exhilarated at the idea of the climb but also a little bit nervous. After all, I had only camped overnight in a tent *once* in my life. What lie ahead was six nights in a tent without a shower, at altitudes I'd never before imagined. I felt like we had trained sufficiently but wasn't certain. The heavy winter snows in Colorado had kept us from being able to train above 10,000 feet and we were going to over 19,000. To say the least, I was apprehensive.

Attempting Mount Kilimanjaro is an exercise in endurance. Our trail was the Machame route. This longer route takes seven days and allows extra time to acclimatize to the high altitudes. Our guides started us at 5,400 feet and we would climb to 19,340 feet over six days. Since John and I live at a higher altitude, 6,000+ feet, we felt we might have an advantage. As we started out, it quickly became evident, based on our oxygen saturation levels and pace, that our assumptions had been accurate. There were 28 in our group, but each day we broke into smaller and smaller groups based on our pace. John and I were generally in the first group to reach camp.

It took us five days to get to the high camp. On the eve when we would begin our summit attempt, our lead guide, Eric, announced that there would be three groups. We were surprised that he didn't assign people to groups. Instead, he let us select for ourselves. This left me and John with only one other person in our group, since everyone else selected either group B or C, each going at a slightly slower pace. At first we were a little sad about our small group—there were people we had climbed with most of the week that we hoped would be a part of our group to the summit. In the end, we realized it was only important that the two of us were together as we struggled to the top.

Our group of three, along with our two guides, was scheduled to leave camp at 11:45 p.m. that night. We had already climbed 3,000 vertical feet over five hours earlier that same day. While it had been the shortest day so far, the lack of rest in between climbs raised some concern about what impact that would have on our summit.

We went to our tents after dinner to attempt sleep. Already dressed in most of my layers and snug in my -20 degree bag, I was comfortable despite the freezing temperature outside the tent. I had no doubt that we were going to make the summit, but I was worried about the cold—it was below zero with wind chill. My stomach was rumbling like the San Andreas Fault during an earthquake, a typical reaction to high altitude as the body tries to purge.

During the previous two days we had all become acutely aware of this natural phenomenon, as everyone took their turns using the portable toilet facilities. Until then, no one had understood or been prepared for this very "normal" way the body takes care of itself when it is deprived of oxygen. At altitude, the body shuts down systems to focus energies on respiration and maintain core body heat. Climbing to higher and higher elevations, our bodies needed to purge all that they held. Bathroom talk, which none of us would usually engage in, became part of our group conversation. That evening before the summit climb, I couldn't sleep. The knowledge that my body was still in "purging mode," as well as the anticipation of the endeavor ahead, kept me awake.

In the darkness, we started off from our high camp situated at 15,500 feet, aided by the light of the waning full moon and our tiny little headlamps. Auguste, our Tanzanian guide, checked my pack and said it was too heavy. Every ounce of weight matters when attempting to climb at high altitude. He asked me for one of my bottles of water and put it in his pack. I secured my pack, stepped in line behind him, and we began our ascent.

Our starting pace seemed pretty brisk compared to some of our other days. Although we had been the last group to head out, we reached the first two groups in the first hour and cheered them on as we passed, picking up our photographer, Jeff, along the way. He managed to "leapfrog" between the groups in order to capture everyone's progress.

Our group of four with our two guides continued up the mountain, and my stomach started to get really angry. I asked if we could stop to go to the bathroom. I wasn't sure if I could do it, but my stomach was telling me I had to try. I have major issues with going #2 if anybody is around, but at this seemingly critical stage I hoped I could let go of my inhibitions. We all headed over to the rocks. Everyone else finished and Jeff stood close by, looking up at the beautiful stars. With his close proximity, my body wouldn't cooperate. I resigned myself to the knowledge that I would simply have to tough it out all the way up the mountain and continue to wrestle with the tiger in my stomach. I hoped I could do it.

I kept my head down most of the time so that my headlamp could shine on the rocks and dirt in front of me. I matched my steps to the steady rhythm of Auguste's orange Viking boots. After a while, our measured pace had a meditative effect and I fell into a climber's trance. At this altitude, you have to put a considerable amount of focus into your breathing in order to take in a sufficient amount of oxygen. This singular focus pushes out all other thoughts from the mind. This may be attuned to the state experienced by Buddhist monks when all but the rhythm of the breath falls away and the mind is completely clear. It was a state of mind I had never before experienced despite meditating for a number of years.

I started to doubt myself somewhere between 16,500 and 17,000 feet. I don't know if this was due to the physiology of high altitude climbing and reduced oxygen levels or just sheer fatigue because I hadn't slept the day before. The mind can start to play tricks on you when it's deprived of oxygen. I wasn't sure I could keep going. My confidence was crumbling. I began to question how I would make it another 2,500 feet. *Could I make it for however many more hours that would entail?* Every breath became a struggle for oxygen and required focused concentration.

My stomach was rolling over and over, and I honestly didn't think I could wait a few minutes, much less a few hours, to go to the bathroom.

I am a very driven and independent person, and I have never liked asking for help. It had never occurred to me until I started climbing that night that I might need help to get to the top of this looming peak, As we continued our ascent, I knew without a doubt that I needed some assistance to make it to the top. It was bitter cold and dark. There is something very isolating about climbing while shrouded in darkness. My trancelike state gave me the sense that I was walking alone on the surface of the moon. The hood on my jacket kept me warm but closed me in from the outside world like a cocoon. There was no reality in the moment other than the pain in my lungs and the howling wind. We were in a single-file line, so even if I had spoken and asked for some kind of assistance, I knew the wind would have blown the words away without them being heard. I felt John's love and support behind me giving me strength, but I didn't want to stop and share my doubts with him or ask for some type of additional encouragement. I knew losing any momentum might prevent us both from reaching the top and I didn't want to let him down. I sensed that I needed a different kind of help.

As I struggled with each step, I began to think of my parents. They had always been so proud of everything I'd accomplished in life. My mother passed away in 2006 and my father in 2007. Before the trip, I thought about how proud they would have been of me for supporting John on this climb. At this point, when I really needed guidance and support, my parents came to mind again, but my very next thought was that they couldn't really help me.

As my reserves dwindled, my eyes filled with tears and I asked them to please come and help me make it up the mountain. This was an especially odd request since my mother had multiple sclerosis and hadn't been able to walk during the last 20 years of her life. As soon as I made my silent plea, I felt my parents, one on each side, reach under my arms and lift me up. My vision blurred with tears, but I felt lighter and lighter with each subsequent step. I knew that the power of their love, even beyond death, would carry me onward to the summit.

I also remembered a prayer my mother used to say all the time, "I can do all things through him who comforts me." I began to recite that little prayer in my head over and over with each step. It took my mind off the difficulty ahead and amazingly made it much easier to go on. I am not religious in a formal sort of way, but I was in awe at how much this simple prayer, along with the support of my parents, was able to lighten my burden and get me up the mountain. With each step, I knew I was getting a little closer to the summit and I felt a little bit better.

I regained some spring in my step as we made our way up the steep incline to Stella Point where we stopped for a break before our final hour push to the top. It was still quite dark as we reached Stella at 18,815 feet. John had been climbing right behind me all along but had no idea about the battle that had gone on in my heart on the way up. When we reached this point—so close to the top— we knew the summit would be ours. I burst into tears and turned to him.

"Did you ever think nine years ago when you were

diagnosed with Parkinson's that the two of us would be standing on this peak now?"

His eyes misted as he nodded his head. No, he couldn't have imagined it either. We both cried at the enormity of this accomplishment and the hope it represented. Our group then sat for a few minutes, drinking hot water in the bitter cold wind, before "soldiering on" for the last hour to the top. Our pace slowed, and we wobbled in our steps as we struggled to the summit.

We reached the peak at sunrise and watched as the tiny pin of light burst across the horizon. Once again, I was overwhelmed with emotion at our accomplishment. At first, I didn't recognize what I was feeling. Now, I understand that it was pure joy. I had never felt so alive despite my physical exhaustion. I was overwhelmed with love for being alive.

Summiting Kilimanjaro helped me truly understand the meaning of love—the love that lingers long after someone you love ceases to breathe, the depth of love that strength and encouragement between two partners brings, and most of all, the love and gratitude for the life that I have on this tiny little ball called Earth.

Love is everywhere when we open our hearts to notice.

Martha Carlin is an adventurer, real estate consultant, entrepreneur and writer. She lives in Parker, Colorado with her husband John, three children and two golden retrievers, where she volunteers with Compassion in Action and SCORE. Martha loves to garden and cook— both passions she got from her parents. She was born in Frankfort, Kentucky, graduating from the University of

Kentucky with a BS in Accounting. Her blog "Reflections on Going through Life" can be found at www.marthacarlin. com, where you can find a day-by-day accounting of the climb up Kilimanjaro along with other musings. She expects to release her first novel, The Seeds, in the summer of 2013. Adventures on the horizon include Mt. Rainier and a section hike up the Appalachian Trail in 2013 as well as Nepal's Annapurna Circuit and Chulu Peak in 2014.

True and Forever

Tina Liebetrau

I THINK GOD SPEAKS TO US IN DIFFERENT WAYS, and if you are not hearing the message He is sending, He just speaks louder until you do. In my case, I kept hearing about Lori Schneider through friends in several different areas of my life. After I heard Lori speak for the second time in two months, the light bulb finally went off in my head. I knew I was going to climb Mt. Kili with this wonderful group.

Mt. Kili was a turning point in my life. Since that time, I have stopped saying "when I retire" and started living *now*. I continue to step outside the box and my comfort zone to try new things.

On Kili I formed friendships that are true and will last forever with people who also stepped out of their comfort zones. I saw the strength in each individual with MS or PD. Every person fought hard to make it up the mountain. We laughed along the way and became a family.

I thank God that He spoke so loud, and I am grateful that I heard His call. My life is forever enriched by this experience.

Tina Liebetrau, *CPA and adventure seeker. Janesville, Wisconsin. You can reach Tina at liebetrau@charter.net.*

The Voice of the Mountain

"The earth does not belong to us.
We belong to the earth."
- Chief Seattle

The Experience of No

Mickey Babcock

"NO."

The word was clear, spoken with a female voice… not an angry voice, but an important one. But who was speaking? After all, I was high upon Mount Kilimanjaro and preparing to make the final climb to the summit. There was only a male Tanzanian guide near me, but in the dark **her** voice said "no." I listened and turned around on the path to head back to base camp.

My journey to the highest point in Africa was done… or was it? That moment, at once spiritual and profound, was the reason I was on this trip. I just didn't know it then and am only beginning to understand it now, more than a year after the climb. I have not been able to write or express my feelings until now…a sense of shame has followed me since then. I don't believe it is shame for not reaching the summit (which some climbers may feel); I believe I feel shame because in my limited human way, I am not able to understand. I know for certain that I have experienced something that is both spiritual and very significant for my life.

When Lori Schneider strode onto the stage in Jackson Hole some time ago, I was mesmerized by her strength and grace. As she spoke, she shared her experiences of reaching the summit of all seven of the world's highest peaks, while living with multiple sclerosis. After her presentation, there was nothing that could stop my desire to join her and her team as they made their "Leap of Faith." I was thrilled to have been selected as a companion climber to Susie Weber, who lives with MS, to make the journey to the top of Kilimanjaro. Months of preparation led to our journey, and I met our team in the days before our ascent began.

Africa is a spiritual land. I had prepared my mind and body as best I could for the climb; however, there is no substitute for **feeling** the sacred land of Africa—touching the soil, smelling the air, hearing the silence among the noise. Africa is alive with a connection to the realm of the unknown that is beyond most human understanding. Clearly, there is significant history in Africa; but the deeper knowing is the real story.

Our assembly to make this climb was outstanding. The climbers, those living with disease and those who partnered with them, were an inspirational group. The support team—guides (American and Tanzanian), porters, and cooks—made the journey very comfortable. Yet, for me, there was a sense of guilt: *too many feet* upon this sacred mountain, too many feet. We were over 100 in our group, and the groups around us numbered as many. *What is the environmental impact of that many feet, that much garbage, that much noise? How does this impact the sacred mountain?* I wondered.

After days of ascending, the evening of the summit approach arrived. With much anticipation and some reservation, the team accepted our responsibilities and prepared for the culmination of the journey—to summit Mount Kilimanjaro by the first light of day. For some, this was the beginning of a new way of living; for others, it was the beginning of a new life. I fell into the latter group.

I worked my way up the mountain toward the summit until my body shook uncontrollably—not from cold, but from some sense of "wrongdoing." I could not maintain a focus, and I knew I was entering a zone of altitude illness. It was then that the voice spoke. NO. Only once, but once was enough. I turned toward base camp, slept, and awaited the arrival of the other team members—those who had indeed made the summit.

I have never regretted my choice to return to base camp that night. I believe it was not my purpose to be with my partner and this extraordinary team to reach the summit, but rather to be with these wonderful souls as I was guided to hear the sacred. I believe I was meant to offer a space of awareness and love for both the mountain and the climbers. I believe I was meant to open the pathway for the dialogue that must begin. How do we honor our dreams while honoring the earth? How do we honor our lives as well as the lives of those who live in such sacred lands? When is it appropriate to say no? There is power in being near those who live with **"no"**—no, as in physical restrictions from disease; no, as in cultural biases and economic segregation; no, as in no more environmental degradation.

I hope I learn this lesson of **NO**. I trust that I will be given the opportunity to make my own "Leap of Faith." I am grateful and humbled by the gift. Thank you.

Mickey Babcock lives in Jackson, Wyoming, and is the founder of The Equipoise Fund, a private charitable foundation which focuses resources toward social-economic justice for the women and girls of Wyoming. Mickey lived much of her life in Memphis, Tennessee, but now finds the Rocky Mountains to be her true home. Her family includes Zeke, Cyrus, and her stepchildren.

A Different
Kind of Summit

Monique Giroux

JUST PUT ONE FOOT IN FRONT OF THE OTHER.
One step, then another. This is the message I tell myself as
I look up toward the mountaintop. Although I can't yet see
the summit, I can feel the energy of the hikers moving their
way toward what now seems like an endless goal.

Each step is so arduous that I wonder how the team is
doing. As a doctor, neurologist, and specialist in treating
movement disorders, I often wonder how it must feel when
one's body struggles with the simplest of movements. I think
about this as I struggle to pick up my feet and consider for
a moment that I am beginning to understand and feel, at
least on some level, the physical struggle that I treat as a
doctor each day.

The moon shines over my left shoulder, and I need to
remind myself to look up after every few steps to preserve
the memory. I fight the urge to stop. I wonder how I will
feel if I can't keep up, if I do not make it to the top. *Just one
more step.*

Our guides begin to sing in beautiful a cappella style.
"Kilimanjaro, Kilimanjaro. Mlima mrefu sana…" Their

melodic voices, complemented by the full moon, seem to ignite the spirit of the mountain and the climb, as well as my own spirit and—I imagine—the inner spirit of my fellow companion climbers. Our guides, whose job it is to see that we climb safely and successfully, often putting their own comfort aside, seem to know intuitively that we need their help in that moment. I feel that we are all in this together and our collective energy will move us upward.

My next step is not unlike the one before yet in many ways quite different. It feels a little lighter, a little stronger, and a little more confident. Just when I am ready to give up and go no farther, I take the next step and find I have the strength to keep going. I discover unexpected beauty in that next moment. That is the gift of Kilimanjaro.

The beauty of this moment is my most vivid and cherished memory of the entire climb, even though it lasted less than ten minutes, a mere fraction of the six days and nights we spent on the mountain. In that instant, my doubts, fears, and desires took a backseat as I felt a true kinship with the mountain, our guides, and companion climbers.

This climb, this group of individuals, each with their own story, their own struggles, fears, dreams, and aspirations, are here to leave a mark and to make a difference. Some are here to conquer the mountain rather than sit on the sidelines, proving to themselves and the world that they have so much more to offer than their disease might imply. For others, the need to belong and feel whole again attracted them to this mountain with its sense of adventure, its strength, and its beauty. And for all of us, the desire to reach out to others and experience the trek together brought us to Kilimanjaro.

Kilimanjaro was (and still is) a healing experience. There is a feeling of strength that comes over me with the sight of this mountain, the highest free-standing mountain in the world. As a physician, I have spent the past 20 years, and too many hours to count, studying disease, its treatment, and prevention. Western medicine, with its emphasis on disease and cure, is quick to define a person as *sick* or *well*, *broken* or *whole*. More often than not, physicians also define themselves using a similar dichotomy characterized by their own success in "making their patients well or less broken." When dealing with a progressive neurologic disease, how does this line of thinking enable a physician to treat and a patient to heal? Healing starts by throwing aside these preconceived ideas and societal assumptions— refusing to focus on disability over ability. Even when living in the face of disease and sometimes as a result of disease, some people grow stronger. This strength occasionally shows itself physically, but more often it shows in spirit and compassion.

When asked by my colleague Sierra Farris to join her on the climb as medical support, I was hesitant. Can the group do it? Will we be safe? What unknowns will we face accompanying a group of individuals with neurologic disorders on a high-altitude trek? As I listened to this inner voice, I realized that I was responding to the fear of the unknown and working off those same preconceived ideas and assumptions that my patients face.

I joined the group not just to support our climbers living with MS or Parkinson's, but in a small way, to show support for each and every one of my patients and, for that matter, the neurologic community at large. I hoped to be able to scream out from the mountaintop that it is the person and how they chose to live in the moment that counts. Not how graceful they move, how fast they go, or their level of muscular power. I wanted to shout that living in fear for one's future invites fear into the moment. That it is our inner rather than outer strength that makes a difference. That we have what it takes to all live well. For me, the mountain and the journey now symbolize the power of intention, the resiliency of spirit, and the potential for compassion.

I believe the climb held a similar ideal for many of my fellow climbers. Our leader, Lori Schneider, showed us that even Mt. Everest can be climbed by will, determination, belief in one's self, and hard work. Lori put these ideals to the test as she trained for Mt. Everest on a hill 300 feet high in the otherwise flat terrain of Wisconsin.

Climbing a 19,000-foot mountain is no small feat. It is an even greater challenge if you have muscle rigidity, spasms, coordination difficulties, blurry vision, numbness in your feet or hands, and fatigue. Our climbers with MS and Parkinson's showed tremendous strength in spirit and character as they took on the challenge, despite symptoms sure to make the trek much harder and perhaps more uncertain. Questions remained as to whether they could make it to the top, how they would feel if they did not, and how their symptoms would behave at high altitude. This was a big step in conquering the fear of the unknown.

Our companion climbers did not have MS or Parkinson's, but their commitment, contribution, and achievement was no small affair either. Admiration comes to mind when I think of the companion climbers. Our companions were there to offer support to the MS and Parkinson's climbers. Some did not have a family member with MS or Parkinson's and had not previously met the other team members. They joined the team simply to offer what they could through their support. Their presence truly was an unselfish act of kindness. To hear their heartfelt stories about their own experience on the climb and what it meant to be a part of this team reminds me that kindness and compassion, when given from the heart, will be reflected back.

The mountain was a level playing field. The companions and support team—myself included—revealed our own vulnerabilities and ultimately needed as much support as we intended to give. Not everyone got to the top but everyone summited in reaching a new acceptance of themselves, a renewed sense of self-empowerment, an appreciation for life's precious moments, and the power of intention and community.

Every climber experienced the disappointment of setting their sight on the top of the mountain only to learn it was a false summit. The true summit is yet to come. It may even be out of reach. But what one learns about oneself along the way is always within our grasp.

For me, as a physician, this journey was about reaching a different kind of summit. When I reflect on this trip, I realize my true summit was about 2,000 feet below the mountaintop, in the very moment that our guides connected us to each other and to the mountain with their song. It is not about being an amazing diagnostician (like the doctors depicted on popular TV medical shows) or whether I can successfully treat symptoms of disease or publish the latest scientific breakthrough. It is about being present enough to find those healing moments and support my patients as they reconnect with their inner strength and spirit, and to do so with humility and compassion.

Monique Giroux *is a physician with specialty training in neurology, movement disorders and integrative medicine from Yale, Emory University and the University of Arizona. Upon returning from Africa, Dr. Giroux and fellow climber, Sierra Farris, PAC, opened the Movement & Neuroperformance Center of Colorado in Englewood, Colorado. More information is available at http://www. centerformovement.org/. This unique center brings the spirit of the Mt. Kilimanjaro climb to the neurology community through inspiration, personal healing and empowerment. She continues to hike and climb, using her time in the mountains to reflect on the beauty and important things in life.*

Wild African game, in all its glory, roams the spectacular parks of Tanzania throughout the Great Rift Valley, delighting our eyes and warming our hearts.

We experience the animal kingdom in a way few have ever seen, on our dramatic sunrise balloon safari over the Serengeti Plains.

The soft glow of a late night tent competes with the glow from the stars above.

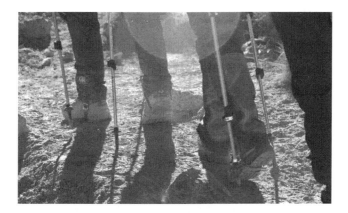

Hiking the dusty trails of the Machame route on ascent and the Mweka route on descent, we live our dream...one step at a time.

We pass the famous Breach Wall, the largest ice and rock face in Africa, nicknamed "The Icicle."

The dynamic duo, 79-year-old Neal Schneider and daughter Lori climb Kilimanjaro together for a second time, 18 years after their first summit in 1993, on Neal's 61st birthday.

Summit of Kilimanjaro-July 18, 2011
Leap of Faith MS, PD, companion climbers,
and medical team make history!

Our porters from the Chagga Tribe, indigenous to the slopes of
Kilimanjaro, are an integral part of our African journey, providing
support, knowledge, and friendship.

Climbing beyond the boundaries of our neuro-degenerative diseases and perceived limitations is a mountainous task.

This stone cairn, a symbol of endurance and strength, guides us along our path.

Husband and wife team, John and Martha, give hope and inspiration to those living with Parkinson's disease.

All for one and one for all, as this PD team stands stronger together. Nathan lives with Parkinson's and has two deep brain stimulators implanted to control his once debilitating tremors. Support companion Daniel's own father lives with PD, so his journey has special meaning.

Climbers seek protection from the sun, wind, and dust by wearing protective facemasks, hats, and boot gaiters.

Ines, Brandis, and Stephanie, an MS trio of hope and inspiration.

Breathe in, breathe out...Sarah's cry of triumph and joy.

68-year-old Connie summits for a second time, 49 years after her first
Kili climb at age 19. She shares the flag with first-time mountaineer,
Ines from Spain, and trip leader, Lori. A joyous moment for all!

It is More than a Mountain;
it is our journey of self-discovery and empowerment.

39 miles,
7 days,
25 pounds,
19,340 feet,
23 years
old, MS

Elation at elevation

Cocooned in her sleeping bag for warmth, April makes the epic two-day, jarring eight-mile traverse down the rocky terrain in a gurney. April lives with secondary progressive MS, and climbed to an amazing 16,500 feet, along with her climbing partner Jeanne.

Hi ho, Hi ho! It's off to work we go. Seven days of hiking, scrambling, climbing, slipping, sliding, tripping, falling, getting up, dusting off, and doing it all over again the next day, with a smile on each of our faces.

A sea of clouds float beneath 14,977 ft. Mt. Meru in Africa. It is truly a sight to behold.

Crowned by eternal snows, the mighty Kilimanjaro at 19,340 ft. is the highest free-standing mountain in the world and dominates its landscape unlike any other mountain. Located in Tanzania, this extinct volcano looms over five eco-systems and large game reserves and is certainly one of the world's most impressive sights.

We begin our Kilimanjaro quest at the Machame Gate, jumping off point for our monumental Leap of Faith. 10 with MS, 4 with PD, 14 companions including medical experts, 2 western guides, 11 Tanzanian guides, 136 porters, and 1 fabulous photographer…we are ready!

These photos and more are available for purchase online at www.jeffrennicke.com

Afterword

ONE YEAR AFTER OUR JOURNEY UP THE MOUN-
tain, we held a reunion in Estes Park, Colorado, with
about 75 percent of the climbers in attendance. It was an
opportunity to reconnect, share our insights, deepen our
relationships, and even attempt to resolve unanswered
questions.

There are times and circumstances when we cannot
answer all the questions. We oftentimes attempt to answer
them through our own narrow looking glass, assuming we
know what others are thinking. Reading these stories let
me know in so many ways that I had no idea what others
had been thinking. Each experience was unique. The steps
on the trail may have been the same but the personal
journeys were not in any way identical. For some, the
journey was triumphant, for others it was an opportunity to
define what it means to reach one's personal summit. For
all, this journey allowed us to learn something more about
ourselves and each other.

For many, the Leap of Faith journey up Kilimanjaro was
the trip of a lifetime, both geographically and experientially.

I was struck, after reading my fellow climbers' deeply personal stories, by the struggles each person had on the mountain. These were quiet struggles, never shared in the meal tent at the end of the day, nor during the many quiet hours on the hiking trails or sitting on the porch throughout our reunion weekend.

Some of the struggles were physical but many were psychological. Some of us found something on the mountain; others of us left something behind. Some are going on to climb bigger mountains—Sarah and Sean will climb Aconcagua in South America December 16, 2012 hoping to summit on January 1st, 2013. Their continued resolve and positive attitudes are a great inspiration.

Maybe more of us will climb together again; maybe we won't. We will, however, continue to encourage and inspire each other to reach beyond what we used to think was possible. We have Lori Schneider to thank for lighting that spark in all of us. Lori has been an inspiration to people around the world, having climbed the Seven Summits. Her personal support and inspiration to each member of this group provided a perfect example for how to live our lives—give of your time, teach your wisdom, inspire hope, and above all else, share your love.

November 2012
Martha Carlin

for Gina Anderson and the
Empowerment Through Adventure program's 2011 Kilimanjaro expedition

More Than a Mountain

lyrics adapted from the poem by
Josie Baughman

Brandon Nelson
ASCAP

More than a Mountain Theme Song Credits

Gina Anderson
Kilimanjaro teammate
living with MS
Creative Musical Director
for More than a Mountain

Suz Thomson
Kilimanjaro companion
climber for Gina Anderson
Vocals for More than a Mountain

Acknowledgements: More than a Mountain
Talents donated by the following friends:
Composed by Brandon Nelson
Lyrics adapted from the poem by Josie Baughman
Acoustic Guitar by Bryce Thomson
Keyboard/Rhythm by Manfred Schonauer
Sound Mix by Steve Vogt
Recorded in Pipe Dream Center, Comstock, WI
Cover by Joe Routhier

Additional song on CD titled FanFare for the Women
Composed by Libby Larsen
Trumpet by Gina Anderson
Inside Jacket Artwork by Susie Weber

Acknowledgments

Thank you to our 'Book Inspiration Team', Martha Carlin, Suz Thomson, Sarah Conrad, and Gina Anderson, for believing in the power of our journey and helping to share our stories with the world.

To Jeff Rennicke for documenting our adventure through his compelling words and photographs.

To Susie Weber for her artistic graphic design and artwork.

To Gina Anderson, Suz and Bryce Thomson, and many musical friends, for the creation of our *More than a Mountain* theme song.

To our expert guides at Alpine Ascents for helping us reach our goals.

To our dedicated medical volunteers, Dr. Monique Giroux and Sierra Farris-PA, who helped heal us inside and out.

A special thanks to Seattle's REI for providing shirts to the Leap of Faith climbers.

To team leader Lori Schneider for believing in each one of us and reminding us all of our inner strength.

To 79 year old climber Neal Schneider, who reminded us all that you are never too old to live your dreams.

To our families, friends, and all those who supported our efforts, making this leap a reality for so many.

To the entire Leap of Faith team, for your incredible efforts in changing the world's perceptions about what is possible for people with a neurodegenerative disease.

A mountain of thanks to all of you.

"This watercolor was created just for this MS Kilimanjaro trip as the banner for my blog. The stars, symbolic of the climbers with MS & PD and confetti, representing the companion climbers, sponsors and our supporters...all celebrating and climbing Mt. Kilimanjaro. If you look hard, you may also find one heart and a musical note. Mountains are such great metaphors I can truly say that living with MS myself is like climbing a mountain, every single day."

— SUSIE WEBER, ILLUSTRATOR